MAN ON THE RUN

MAN ON THE RUN

A Collection of Trail Running Stories

From Manitoba to Mount Everest

Mark Timmons

ISBN - 978-1-7776344-0-7

Printed by Leech Printing Ltd.
Brandon, Manitoba

To Breanne, Heather, and Logan,

and Sharon, of course!

"To see ourselves defined

By all we embrace"

-Love Shines,

Ron Sexsmith

Table of Contents

Acknowledgments *viii*

Preface *x*

Nepal, May 29, 2014 1

Let Me Introduce to You…Kilian the Great! 3

The Pursuit of Greatness 6

More Than a Feeling 14

Lessons From Leadville 17

Seven Sins 29

Eyes Frozen Shut 42

Laz's Laps 51

The Call of Kilian 56

Heaven and Hell on Hamperokken 60

I Think I'm Going to Kathmandu 74

A Guide and His Umbrella 82

Kerosene Eggs 92

The Bowels of Base Camp 98

Blinded by the Light 105

Yak Sadness 111

Yak Happiness 117

Back to Mong and Beyond 125

Why It All Matters 129

Ultra Distancing 141

Afterword *152*

Acknowledgments

A big thank you must first go out to Cam, Colleen, Tyler, and James at A & L Cycle in Brandon, Manitoba, Canada, for their financial support in helping to get this book published; without them, it would have remained nothing more than my own private diary.

To Donna Lowe and Dennis Rogers, thank you for the contributions you have made through your masterful command of the English language. I have spent my entire adult life speaking the language of the Periodic Table and distilling real-world physics problems into mathematical equations. Consequently, my first attempt at writing a book was a bit of a messy endeavour. Without your editing skills, this project would have never come to fruition.

When looking back at my favourite travel and adventure books, I have always appreciated the author's dedication to sharing the full experience by including photographs. A huge thank you to Mark Phinney, for his generosity, and his dedication and skill in helping me illuminate my adventures by adding some of my most cherished photographs to this book.

Kevin Grindey: Ever since our walk in the woods together as teaching colleagues several years ago, when I first told you about my adventure in Nepal, you have been an enthusiastic supporter of my writing and storytelling. Your interest in my adventures has, in all honesty, been my inspiration for completing this book and sharing it with others. Thank you for all your encouragement. It has been great getting to know you as friend during this time.

Just as with Kevin, Lindsay Kendall is someone that I have also known as a respected colleague and now think of as a friend. From the beginning, you have always supported my efforts to share memories of my adventures in writing, and your comments inspired me to keep on writing. Thank you.

And finally, I want to express my gratitude to the incredible group of students that I had the pleasure to teach, and get to know personally, during my last five years at Neelin High School in Brandon. Part of my inspiration in seeking out running adventures was the inspiration I gained from you.

Spending my working life in your presence encouraged me to seek out fulfillment in my personal life. Sharing my passion for adventure with you helped to motivate me to become a better teacher, a more sensitive listener and a more compassionate friend. Thank you for being with me on this journey; I will always remember you.

Preface

Walk into any bookstore these days and it would be hard to swing a fuel belt around your head without knocking a running book off the shelf. Inspirational books on marathon running have been around for a long time, but stories about trail running have only become popular during the past few years.

When I started running through mountain trails several years ago, organized races were rare, and virtually nobody I knew of was interested in the sport. Marathon participation had been increasing at a rapid pace for decades, with many runners vying for that elusive Boston Marathon qualifying time, yet trail running was still a niche sport that was generally limited to an exclusive group of skinny hippies and hillbillies. Recently, however, participation in trail running has exploded, and authors and videographers are now producing inspirational stories about men and women in some of the most fascinating and epic adventures the sporting world has ever seen.

As an avid follower of all things running, I have discovered that narratives on the sport of bipedal locomotion generally fall into three categories: awe-inspiring tales of world-class athletes on the path to stardom; training and injury prevention books for novice runners; or the testimonies of people who have discovered running as a means of helping them overcome myriad health or personal struggles. These types of stories are of interest to publishers because, as my own bookshelf can attest, they are of interest to running-inclined readers. However, my time spent among the running community tells me that most runners out there also like sharing stories about their own experiences from the racecourse or trail.

There is great comfort and motivation in genuinely feeling the emotions of that fellow runner who is shedding tears of pain and pride as she struggles through the last few miles of her first long-distance mountain race, or the runner who stops 500 metres from the end of a gruelling marathon to wrap his arms around a fallen competitor and slowly limps with him to the finish, or the runner who bursts into laughter with his wife as she recounts her perils on the mountain trail with a relentless bee swarming around her head.

When I was in Nepal a few years ago to compete in an ultra-marathon at Mount Everest, my group was joined by a celebrity adventure-athlete from Brazil who would be competing in the race with us. He was accompanied by a television crew who were gathering footage for a documentary on the race.

On the eve of our race, this TV crew interviewed me, asking for my thoughts on my Everest adventure. In the interview, I commented that I was just a rather ordinary guy who performs at a rather ordinary level, and that running had provided me with the good fortune to experience some rather extraordinary things.

Thus it is with this book that I have attempted to share with the reader some tales of a post-middle-aged ordinary runner and his pursuit of the extraordinary—and to perhaps inspire others in the running community to see that, as runners, we do not need to be exceptional in order to experience exceptional things.

One

Nepal, May 29, 2014

Leaning over my poles and gasping for oxygen, I looked up through the darkness, trying to focus on the dim light shining from the teahouse at the summit of Mong Hill; in my semi-conscious state, it appeared to be no nearer than the stars above us. My young guide had now been on the trail with me for about six hours and that, coupled with my six hours on the course earlier in the day running solo, meant my goal of finishing the Everest Extreme Ultra-Marathon in twelve hours had now unfortunately passed. But with this distant illumination guiding us up the last major climb on the course, I determinedly, slowly, and methodically pushed my depleted body towards the finish.

Not being able to address my guide by name deterred me from saying much to him at all, and his contribution to our conversations was generally limited to a few kind words spoken in soft broken English: "This way, sir. Slowly, sir." But in this shared silence there had developed a remarkable bond between us, and I know that without him by my side, I would never have overcome the hardships I had battled earlier in the day. I will forever remember him as Ujesh: "one who gives light."

In hindsight, I recognize that this may have been just an ordinary day on the mountain for Ujesh, but the hours we were spending together were becoming anything but ordinary for me. My time with this remarkable young man was having a significant impact on me; perhaps more than any other period in my life. My running life—which is to say my life in general, pretty much—would forever be changed.

There is much more to share about my time with Ujesh, as well as many other stories about my life as an ordinary runner—often in extraordinary places, and always under extraordinary circumstances.

But first…

Two

Let Me Introduce to You...Kilian the Great!

Although running has only recently become a passion of mine, sports in general have always been a big part of my life. I believe most of those who know me would label me as a bit of a sports junkie. I'm not a true junkie like my son-in-law Scott, who could probably cite the successful draw percentage of a Division II college curling team; rather, I am simply a fan of sports at all levels and appreciate a genuine battle between opponents.

But regardless of the sport, what I appreciate and respect the most is greatness. Every sport has its "Great One," be it Gretzky in hockey, Serena in tennis, Bolt in track, or Tiger in golf, and although each of these great athletes suffers defeat occasionally, they possess something special that raises them to a category above all others in their sports.

In the pursuit that has consumed my life over the last ten years, mountain ultrarunning, there is also an athlete whose name is synonymous with greatness. Kilian Jornet, a young Spaniard, has spent his entire life at high elevations climbing, running, and skiing, and as much as I respect all athletes of superior talent and passion, Kilian's accomplishments define an entirely new category of greatness.

I began reading reports of Kilian soon after my introduction to running turned serious about seven years ago. I was a decent marathon runner for my age category but a complete novice to the mountain running scene.

I was in awe of the incredible accomplishments of this young superstar—still just a boy, really—and as the years passed and I became more invested in training and competing in endurance races, my admiration for Kilian continued to grow. Before long I was toeing the start line with some of the best ultrarunners in North America and witnessing how they could push themselves through gruelling long-distance races at extreme altitude, finishing in half my time. This was shocking and humbling, but even more incredible was that these same athletes, when stacked up against Kilian, would consistently finish a distant second.

Two of Kilian's many accomplishments may help to put his greatness in perspective. In the spring of 2017, Kilian summited Mount Everest not once, but twice, within one week—and did this with no supplemental oxygen and no support crew. In Everest mountaineering, this just does not happen!

What makes Kilian's quest even more remarkable is that he is not a professional mountain climber; he just climbs for the challenge and because he can! Later that same summer in Colorado, Kilian won his fourth Hardrock 100, an event that many veterans of the ultrarunning community would classify as the most difficult race in North America, if not the entire planet.

A glance at his finishing time, the slowest of his Hardrock career and just minutes ahead of the second-place finisher, might suggest that claims of Kilian's supreme greatness are unwarranted. However, now consider that while descending a slope just thirteen miles into the race,

Kilian fell and dislocated his shoulder. He struggled to reach the nearest aid station, where his arm was placed in a crude sling, then continued on his way, running overnight through the mountains for an additional eighty-seven miles—with the use of just one arm—to finish ahead of all other world-class runners. Then he waited at the finish line, some twenty hours later, to congratulate the last-place finisher. In the running world, this can only be described as legendary!

KILIAN'S "QUESTS" have been very transformative for me, as they have been to countless others in the global running community. Soon after I discovered Kilian, legions of runners like me started making the transition from the track to the trails—and ultimately to the mountains. As the years went on, interest in trail and mountain running exploded and before long, race calendars were becoming packed with events year-round. Kilian had, almost single-handedly, created a global running phenomenon, to the point where the lure of mountain running to the uninitiated had garnered its own catchphrase: "The Kilian Effect." And I was now being reeled in.

Three

The Pursuit of Greatness

As a child, running held about as much allure to me as mowing the lawn or taking out the garbage; I just never thought of it as something anyone would choose to do for fun. Hockey and baseball occupied most of my time year-round. As I got a bit older, my focus shifted almost exclusively to hockey and as teenage goalie, I worked my way onto a junior team. At the end of my first season, I was called up to play on a team at the highest level of amateur competition and was on my way to a legitimate shot at pursuing hockey as a career.

In my hometown I was a bit of a "Mark of the Moment" and the future looked bright. That was until that cruel affliction called "youth" infected me, and hockey was replaced by friends, girlfriends, and partying. Maturity and marriage ultimately cured me of this youthful abandon, and after ten years of a relative sedentary existence, my passion for hockey returned and I was once again immersed in the camaraderie and competition of the game.

My days at work were consumed by the anticipation of game nights, and when those nights finally arrived the sights, sounds, and smells of the rink were intoxicating. Then, in one of those memorable games, a heavy shot found my knee through a void in my circa-1960 Gump Worsley goalie pads, and in an instant hockey was once again behind me.

I spent the next several years of my life regretting the failings of my youth and desperately craving an opportunity to once again try to be really good at something. Then, as I approached my fiftieth year, I discovered running and realized that my physique and metabolism suited me well for pounding out miles on pavement. I quickly discovered that as a competitor against others of my age I fared reasonably well, and my pursuit for middle-aged greatness was on. Marathon training became my obsession and soon I was competing in several races a year, not all of them intentional.

ONE DAY, WHILE ATTENDING my daughter's wedding in Mexico, I took a break from the pool-side conviviality and went for a run through the streets of Puerto Vallarta. It was late morning and the streets were completely empty. After running in solitude for about an hour, barricades began appearing on the side streets, with small clusters of people standing behind them outside their homes and businesses.

Shortly after, while jogging along at a sun-baked and hungover tourist pace, I heard some unusual sounds behind me, and then suddenly a couple of tall, lean, and very fast runners wearing race bibs blew past me. Soon, I was overtaken by about a half-dozen other runners who appeared to be digging hard trying to catch the two in front of me.

It was then I realized that I had not only stumbled onto the course of the local marathon, but that I had in fact been running all this time ahead of the lead pack, and was now only about one kilometre away from the finish. Once aware that I had unknowingly become a "race bandit," I slid over to the side of the road, trying to make myself less visible to the now cheering fans.

I did decide to continue my run until I reached the finish, where I slowed to a walk and slipped around the finish banner trying not to be mistaken for an actual competitor (and a top ten finisher at that!). However, as I meandered through the tables of finisher medals, water stations, and food stands, my sweat-soaked running singlet and shorts must have made me look very "racer-like," and volunteers began offering me everything from pretzels to prize bags.

After repeated refusals, I eventually grabbed a banana and some chocolate milk and sheepishly sneaked away from the celebration, making sure to take an alternate route back to the resort—where my story of an adventure as the Mysterious Marathon Man brought drunken laughter from the pool-side wedding guests.

IN THE TWO YEARS PRIOR to the wedding, my running had progressed from casual jogs to a rigorous marathon training routine. My training plan was very detailed, and because I was a novice runner, was also one I followed religiously.

In the months leading up to my first marathon, a typical training week would generally follow a transition from several short fast runs ranging from three miles to ten miles to one long and slow run of distances up to twenty-two miles. The fundamental and rather unsophisticated training logic of this plan is that short runs build speed while long runs build endurance.

Success in a marathon is clearly linked to both speed and endurance, but the only real measure of success for a first-time competitor is crossing the finish line and that, above all else, comes from a commitment to NEVER skipping a long run. Thus it was on a warm May morning in Chicago, three weeks out from my first marathon, that I quietly slipped out of my hotel room at 4:00 a.m. to embark on my final long training run of twenty miles through the streets of the Windy City.

I was in Chicago with my colleague Mike and a group of high school science students that we had brought with us to tour some world-class research institutions. In addition to such prestigious facilities as the Fermi Institute of Quantum Physics and the Bio-Robotics Institute at Northwestern University, Mike, a physics teacher, included a trip to the Six Flags Amusement Park in our itinerary for some "applied research" on rotational inertia and gravitational acceleration.

Our thirty-mile train ride to the Park at Gurnee, Illinois departed downtown Union Station at 10:00 a.m., about ninety minutes after I was planning to be back from my run. At about mile fifteen, I started to feel a twinge in my knee. This soon turned into searing pain that migrated up my outer thigh to my hip joint. I was now experiencing my first running injury: a strained iliotibial (IT) band.

My pace over the final five miles slowed considerably, bringing me back to the hotel with barely enough time to shower and catch the train to Gurnee. By this time, I was in a bit of a mess. The inflammation had now turned my leg into a painful stump; I had also consumed very little water and food, and I was extremely tired from being awake and running for the last five hours. Added to this was the fact that I actually hate high-speed spinning rides, and things were not setting up well for a thrilling day at the Park.

We arrived at Six Flags, with lines that were very long, a sun that was blistering hot, and me in a state of flux between puking and fainting. In spite of this, I put on a brave face for my colleagues and the kids and reluctantly followed Mike's lead to the front of the line to hop on our first ride of the day.

Boarding the "Superman" required us to lean forward slightly with our chests resting on a round pad while a second pad moved up under our thighs. Skippy, the seventeen-year-old ride "engineer," then instructed us to stretch our arms out in front of us as a third pad descending from above pushed down on our buttocks. Our bodies were then squeezed into an extended plank and lowered until our faces were barely above the ground.

The next few minutes literally flew by as we were hurled around the American Midwest at Space Shuttle speeds and "g-forces," while I closed my eyes and screamed horrific profanities for the entire duration of the ride. I was more than a little bit ashamed of myself as we disembarked but more concerned for the emotional state of Crystal, our sweet young Korean exchange student, as I'm sure she must have thought her mild-mannered chemistry teacher had transformed into some form of unhinged lunatic before her eyes!

Six more hours of terror and trauma followed as I struggled to walk about the park in a painful, almost comatose state. I quickly became the real source of amusement for the students and they took twisted pleasure in jockeying for a spot beside me on one ride after another, laughing hysterically at my feeble state of body and mind and continued reliance on obscene screams to temper the trauma.

After one final terrifying plunge on the "Death Drop," I quietly limped over to a picnic table in the food court, lay down on my back on top of it with my arms and legs hanging to the ground, and passed out as if I had just quaffed a 12-pack of Budweiser. I was abruptly awakened by the sound of laughter and repeated taps to my face; both kids AND teachers had gathered around me and were taking great pleasure in tossing pieces of french fries and candy corn into my gaping, drooling mouth.

In spite of my frail state of existence, I couldn't help but chuckle to myself as I walked back to the train, knowing that I had provided the kids with as much entertainment and education (the Doppler Effect of roller coater obscenities and the parabolic path of flying carnival foods being just a couple of lessons) as the amusement park itself!

I'VE BEEN BACK TO CHICAGO several times since my adventure with Mike, Crystal, and company and on two occasions, I actually ran in the Chicago Marathon. I feel fortunate to have been able to participate in a few big city marathons; they are quite a spectacle. Chicago is particularly impressive for a number of reasons. It is one of the world's six Marathon Majors (New York, Boston, London, Tokyo, and Berlin being the others), thereby attracting the highest level of competition from across the planet. In both of my races in Chicago, runners in pursuit of world records were in the field, making me feel somewhat like a casual golfer drawing a 9:40 a.m. tee time alongside Tiger Woods in the Masters. Chicago is also one of the largest marathons in the world, with approximately 40,000 runners toeing the start line each year. Once out of the start gate, this sea of runners follow a route that meanders through the iconic and historic city centre as well as through most of the unique and colourful neighbourhoods surrounding the central Loop.

One of these races, in particular, proved to be very meaningful to me for other reasons as well. After I had been running for about twenty-five miles at a comfortable and pain-free pace, my eyes were drawn towards another runner who was lying face down on the pavement with a race medic attending to him. I decided to pull over to the side of the route to enquire about the fallen runner. The medic told me that the man was experiencing serious cramping and fatigue from dehydration, but that he was in no immediate medical danger and could continue if he were able. However, to avoid disqualification this runner would need to complete the race under his own power—only fellow racers could give him assistance to cross the finish line—so I offered to stay by his side. I helped him to his feet, wrapping his arm around my shoulder and placing my own around his waist. Four wobbly legs now moved slowly forward, and eventually we saw the final turn towards the finish line.

Our spirits were immediately lifted. This stretch of pavement presented us with an incredible view of the majestic Chicago skyline while thousands of spectators lined each side of the route, cheering us on as if we were champions. With about one hundred metres to go, we released our embrace and ran side by side, crossing the finish line together. After sharing a hug and a celebratory beer, the two of us parted ways, taking with us perhaps our slowest—yet most memorable—marathon ever.

MY FIRST MARATHON, the Manitoba Marathon in Winnipeg, Manitoba, which followed a few weeks after the trip to Chicago with my students, and a year before my inaugural Chicago Marathon, was especially memorable for a multitude of reasons, but the one that will stick with me (quite literally) occurred about five miles into the race. As a novice, there were many things I needed to discover about long-distance running, one being the amount and variety of food athletes eat while on the course.

I learned that it was typical for aid stations along the route to have various soft drinks, cookies, and candy available to provide much-needed calories for the runners. Experienced runners also told me that it was not uncommon for fans along the route to hand out extra goodies such as Smarties, gummi bears, and Freezies.

Thus I was not surprised when, early in the race, a man on the street handed me a long tongue depressor coated in a large dollop of honey. I grabbed the stick, placed it in my mouth, and wrapped my tongue and teeth around it, trying to gather every bit of sweetness.

Instantly, the odd texture and absence of flavour made it clear that I was not eating honey, but rather a thick glob of viscous Vaseline. In my ignorance, I did not realize that the "honey" was intended to be smeared on nipples, armpits, and crotches to prevent chafing.

I spent the rest of the race, a full three hours, spewing sticky bitumen from my mouth. Vaseline is immiscible in saliva—you just can't spit it out—so along with ineffective expectorating, I regularly scraped the sputum off my teeth and tongue with my finger and wiped it on my shirt and shorts. Needless to say, I was in a bit of a soiled state by the time I hobbled to the finish.

It was indeed a slow, messy, exhausting, and painful experience, but completing this race for the first time made me realize that with proper training, I could both improve my performance and enjoy the experience much more. When I returned three years later to run the same race, I was able to meet the Boston Marathon qualifying time; from my state of despondent resignation a few years earlier, when I considered my life as an athlete to be over, I was now accepted into the field of the world's greatest marathon.

Four

More Than a Feeling

And what an epic marathon Boston turned out to be! Record-high temperatures forced organizers to seriously consider cancelling the race, a decision that would have affected over 20,000 runners.

At the eleventh hour, however, race officials decided to start the race as scheduled, with all athletes given the option of not participating and deferring their coveted entry to the following year. It was strongly advised that runners choose the deferral option, as medical officials warned of both impending heatstroke and death.

I felt that this would very likely be my one and only opportunity to run the marathon, so I made the decision to battle the elements and experience Boston at its most demanding. So there I was, at 6:30 a.m. with my then-girlfriend Sharon, waiting for a bus to transport me and about 15,000 other runners to the start line, 26.2 miles outside of downtown Boston. I hopped on the bus while Sharon made her way over to Boylston Street, where she hoped to secure a viewing spot near the finish line.

An unobstructed sightline of the finish is prime real estate on this day, as thousands of fans scramble to cheer on runners when they finish. Sharon realized this, so she had staked out a possible location the night before and hoped that she could arrive early enough to claim that same space on the race route.

At 7:00 a.m., Sharon planted her feet on the exact spot she had coveted and prepared to remain there for the next seven hours. With so many runners in the field, and to alleviate congestion on the narrow roads, Boston uses a staggered start: the elite runners start at 8:00 a.m., whereas my group would be hearing the gun at 10:30 a.m. By the time I started, Sharon had already been standing for three and a half hours with at least that much more time to wait; she somehow managed to suppress any thoughts or urges to grab some food or water or even take a pee break, as vacating her coveted spot was not an option.

Boston is a point-to-point race, so marathoners run east for the entire route. We started late in the morning under a cloudless sky, and the intense New England sun beat down on my face throughout the day. Kind spectators' gestures of water spray guns, lawn sprinklers, and various icy treats—while welcome—did little to suppress the scorching heat. At around mile twenty, and three hours into a very slow race, I took refuge in a portable toilet at the base of the infamous Heartbreak Hill. Despite the offensive conditions, I savoured ten minutes of shade and rest before the push through the final few miles to the finish.

Covered in sunburn and sweat, I eventually struggled to the final turn up Boylston Street, with thousands of fans and police lining the street along the last 200 yards to the finish. As amazing as this sight was, my heart sank as the prospect of finding Sharon in this teeming crowd seemed impossible; and I just had to find her.

Yet, about a hundred yards from the finish line, there she was: exactly in the same spot she had showed me the night before. I veered to my right past the police barricade and embraced Sharon, soiling her with sweat and Gatorade.

"Get to the finish line, Sweetie! Go, Go!" she yelled over the screaming throng of spectators.

At that moment, my life changed forever. I embraced her again, pulled away slightly with her face in my hands, and asked her to marry me!

Yes, I realize that stadium scoreboard and finish line proposals are pretty cheesy, but this moment was symbolic of the beautiful life we had just begun to share together—and I was not about to let the moment pass.

Finishing the Boston Marathon was re-igniting the competitive fire that had been missing since I was a teenager, and I was now absolutely driven to push myself as far as my middle-aged body could take me. I had never felt more exhilarated in my life, knowing that the excitement and physical and mental challenges I was to face in my running future would now be shared.

And all of it would be shared with the most beautiful, most selfless, most supportive, and most compassionate person I will ever know. I am hopeful that whenever my time on this earth comes to an end, my final moments will pass with memories of that April day in Boston.

Five

Lessons From Leadville

My initiation into mountain running actually began one year before Boston, in the small town of Leadville, Colorado. Before meeting Sharon, I read a book called *Born to Run* by Cristopher McDougall, which explored a largely unknown running culture in northern Mexico.

The Tarahumara people of the Copper Canyons are an ancient and secretive society of natural trail runners. For centuries, work and play for the Tarahumara tribes have been intrinsically tied to their minimalistic and highly efficient running style. In the early 1980s, a team of Tarahumara runners was brought to Leadville to compete against the best trail runners in America in the Leadville Trail 100, a one-hundred-mile race across the highest elevation mountain trails in the United States.

Reading about this race made me realize just how much more there was to running than what I was doing at the time. McDougall writes something to the effect that experiencing Leadville is like running back-to-back Boston Marathons without a break, then climbing to the summit of a 12,000-foot mountain…and then turning around to do the same again blindfolded—the entire time trying to breathe with a sock stuffed in your mouth.

At the time, I could hardly believe there were not only world-class athletes running this race, but average runners as well. Pushing through 26.2 miles in daylight on flat pavement seemed like the proverbial "walk in the park" compared to this. How could any human possibly spend up to thirty consecutive hours running through the mountain darkness at 12,000 feet and not succumb to complete physical and mental exhaustion?

I knew at the time that, compared to these athletes, I was in the minor leagues, but I found the setting of Leadville so incredible that I had to go and find out what this extreme world of mountain running was all about.

About six months after we met, Sharon and I made the trip to Colorado, where I hoped to acquire a taste for Leadville and the mountain running experience by participating in the Leadville Trail Marathon, a 26.2-mile race at elevations up to 13,000 feet.

On the first climb upwards on the trail, my lungs could not adapt to the greatly reduced oxygen, and I soon found myself simply walking at a very slow and laboured pace. By the time I struggled to the finish with a seriously strained IT band, I had been in the mountains for about twice as long as my Boston qualifying time. I was completely beat up, yet completely captivated by this mountain culture and couldn't wait to discover more.

Two years later, Sharon joined me once again as I returned to Leadville to run with the big dogs in the real deal: the Leadville Trail 100! Waiting at the start line at 4:00 a.m., the rallying cries of the charismatic race founder Ken Chlouber rang through my head:

"I will commit, I will not quit!"

and

"You are tougher than you think you are...and you can do more than you think you can."

The intense anticipation put my body and soul in a place that I had never known existed. I thought about how far I had come from just a few years before, when puttering around a five-kilometre loop back home made me feel like a carefree kid. The magnitude of what I was now doing was overwhelming. I felt more alive and more energized than ever before, and I could hardly believe that I would be following in the footsteps of so many accomplished runners—and especially the legendary Tarahumara.

By most standards, Leadville is not an overly technical course. What really places Leadville in a level of difficulty beyond most races is that almost the entire one hundred miles is run at elevations above 10,000 feet, with an incredibly steep ascent and descent over the 12,000-foot Hope Pass that must be traversed twice at about the halfway point in the race.

It was during my ascent and descent over this pass that the unique and bizarre world of long-distance mountain running truly revealed itself to me. After two hours of slogging up the front side and surpassing 10,000 feet of elevation, I found the trees thinning to reveal nothing more than rocks, a few blades of grass, and...llamas?

HOPELESS AID STATION is situated just above the tree line and serves as the last opportunity to rest and re-fuel before crossing Hope Pass. Each year, a selfless group of locals pack up about a dozen llamas to help carry their gear up Hope Pass the day before the race. Here, they set up camp on the unforgiving mountainside near the summit, where they party for two days and nights while providing critical care for exhausted runners.

This cadre of twenty or so humans and ungulates serves as an instant energy boost for sunken souls and, in my experience, anyway, stimulates one of two reactions from competitors: for most, their spirits are immediately lifted, and they are enabled to move forward with a renewed focus to "conquer the mountain."

For others, entering this idyllic world of peaceful herbivores grazing in the alpine meadow, along with multiple roaring fires, comfortable tents, and pots of soups, stews, and meatballs worthy of Michelin-starred chefs, reduces their focus into a blissful state of acceptance that their pain and suffering is over, and a sense of resignation that their defeat is justified. As I approached Hopeless Aid station, I witnessed a handful of young tough-looking mountain men in front of a fire, wrapped in blankets and leaning back in lawn chairs with beverages in hand, sporting oddly contented "I'm Done!" smiles. I imagined a John Denver impersonator could have been sitting in one of those chairs strumming an old acoustic and crooning out the lyrics to "Rocky Mountain High."

I MOVED ON FROM THIS TRANQUIL SCENE, but upon returning from the fifty-mile turn-around at the base of the back side of Hope Pass, I was in a seriously depleted mental and physical state. The thin air, extreme heat, inadequate food and water, and the punishing terrain were all taking their toll on me.

I climbed at a ridiculously slow pace up a 2000-foot wall of scree-covered switchbacks, trying not to lean back and tumble to the valley floor below. Gazing up at the remaining trail to the summit was psychologically traumatizing. I resorted to simply closing my eyes, dropping my head, and leaning into my poles, pushing through one painful step after another—mountain somnambulating, one might call it!

Suddenly, I was shaken from my semi-conscious state by a horrendous sound from above. Not a rockslide, not a wild beast, but rather a fellow runner, hunkered down behind a tree the size of a trekking pole, and evacuating himself in the most foul and most excruciating way imaginable.

The vertical faces surrounding us provided an acoustic amphitheater that only amplified this poor guy's intestinal distress. Horrific, painful wails accompanied relentless spasms as he involuntary expunged the day's nutrients. Cycles of intense vomiting and diarrhea were followed by faint whimpers of "I'm so sorry!"

The compassion and camaraderie of the mountain revealed itself, as one by one passing runners offered words of comfort to their fallen fellow competitor: "It's OK, pal, been there, just let it go" or "Hey, no problem buddy, we're on the trail, shit happens!"

As brutal as I was feeling on that day, it was nothing compared to this unfortunate soul's plight, and that fact actually lifted my spirits. I felt terrible for this guy, but I couldn't help but laugh out loud at his pathetic predicament, and was thankful it wasn't me behind that spindly Charlie Brown tree, curled up against a rock soiled by my own waste. I can't think of another sport where sublime inspiration and primal misery co-exist so vividly!

Shortly after, I witnessed another moment that reminded me of the truly unique environment I was in. At the halfway point in the race, runners are allowed to enlist the assistance of a pacer for the remaining fifty miles. Pacers are often used by competitive runners who either require—or simply desire—a friend to remain by their sides through the most demanding part of the race, providing physical and emotional companionship. Because pacers also have to cover fifty miles of the race, they must be skilled and experienced mountain runners themselves as well as function as the ultimate support crew. Simply put, by this point in the race, your pacer had better be in much better shape than you are.

There were many runner/pacer teams around me on this day and for the most part, I was quite envious of them. I couldn't help but imagine how great it would be to have a capable, trusting, and caring mate beside me pushing me to continue. Then a runner with his pacer passed me and it soon became apparent that pacers are not all they are cracked up to be.

As this team moved up the mountain, I observed them stopping with ever-increasing frequency. Then I noticed the runner moving up the mountain alone, with no pacer at his side. Once again, the cacophony of sounds from renegade bodily functions filled the air as the pacer succumbed to the stresses of the environment, fell onto a large rock, and started puking with power.

His runner would then stop and wait for this incompetent sidekick to catch up before the pacer would once again need to find purchase against a rock to rest for minutes at a time. I knew that my slow pace would bring me to the next checkpoint perilously close to a time cut-off, so clearly this runner was in the same predicament. As had been the case a few minutes earlier, being witness to the struggles of others provided me with a brief moment of strength and inspiration (if not a few chuckles!) and I pushed towards the summit with renewed focus.

I am not one to wish ill will upon anyone, especially those experiencing the same, if not worse, pain than I was. Nonetheless, moments like those I had just witnessed would make even the most empathetic and compassionate runner smile a bit; it's just a very strange —and yet very real—part of long-distance mountain running.

***

AND CLEARLY, suffering in long-distance races does not apply just to men; women crash and burn just as often, and just as spectacularly as men do. I give you two examples of this.

I have a friend who recently returned from a running and hiking trip along the high elevation trails in Nepal, and she wrote to me describing a painful and debilitating condition that often afflicts high altitude climbers, trekkers, and runners.

Conditions such as HAPE (High-Altitude Pulmonary Edema), and HACE (High-Altitude Cerebral Edema), are well-known and very serious conditions, but what she experienced was something totally new. As she was trekking through the highest elevations on her trip, she started experiencing repeated bouts of extreme flatulence. Unknown to her, she had developed a severe case of HAFE (High-Altitude Flatus Expulsion)—a condition described by American physician Paul Auerbach as a "gastrointestinal syndrome which involves the spontaneous passage of increased quantities of rectal gases at high altitudes."

Not potentially deadly like both HAPE and HACE, but HAFE can, and apparently did, cause her to suffer extreme discomfort to the point where she could no longer move; she had literally farted herself to the point of pain and exhaustion. Certainly not the kind of issue you would see on a volleyball court or in a swimming pool.

ANOTHER RUNNER, Katie Azmuth, reported on her Instagram account about a rather unusual traumatic event that happened to her on the trail. While running in the lead of an ultramarathon, she tripped and fell face first into a rock. When she got to her feet and began tracing her fingers over her battered face, she realized that she had broken her nose, which was bleeding heavily.

Somehow, she managed to stay in the lead, continuing to run until she arrived at the next aid station. A medic attended to her wounds by wiping the blood off her face and then staunching the flow by…stuffing a tampon into her bleeding nostril. The tampon remained in her nose for rest of the race (several hours), where she crossed the finish line as the champion. Toughness is definitely not the exclusive domain of men!

So it is not uncommon that in situations like these, or those in Leadville, trail runners laugh at others who find themselves in these predicaments, just as they laugh at themselves. There is certainly care for other runners on the trail, but there is definitely no coddling; in a strange way, joking about things like broken noses and angry guts is a sign of respect, and an acknowledgement that trail runners are warriors.

Heck, even the race doctor at Leadville made light of trail trauma in his briefing to us the day before our race:

"Ok racers, now listen up. You'll be running for a day or more at extremely high elevations. You'll need to drink regularly, as dehydration can be a real issue. At times, you may feel dizzy and possibly nauseous. And if that happens, just pull over to the side of the trail and puke! C'mon, you're not gonna die from throwing up!"

Hope Pass was making it very clear to me that in races like Leadville, the mountain levels the playing field for everyone. We are all in the same "sufferfest" together.

GENDER EQUALITY ON THE TRAILS goes well beyond pain and humiliation. At any level of competition, and in any sport, injuries and accidents affect all athletes. But what places ultrarunning in a unique category among most sports is that women and men consistently battle for the top spot, in the same event. In long-distance races throughout the world, female runners are placing higher and winning races more than ever before, and product sponsorship and media coverage of women runners rivals that of men. Pay equity, unfortunately, still has some catching up to do; in some races, men's purses are still higher than women's. This is changing, however, as at least one world-class runner (my friend Ruth, whom you will meet later), has exposed this inequity by publicly boycotting prestigious events where prize money for the top male finishers is higher than it is for the top female finishers.

I have often thought that Olympic organizers should include ultrarunning as a medal sport, with NO gender divisions. Imagine the interest in an Olympic event where the best athletes in the world were just that: athletes.

I can further imagine the excitement as the CBC broadcasters call the final moments of a one hundred-mile race:

"Welcome, viewers from across Canada to Chamonix, France, and the 2024 Summer Olympic Games. I'm Brian Williams, along with Ailsa MacDonald, champion and record holder at the Sinister 7 mountain race in Alberta."

"So Ailsa, it says here in my notes that Sinister 7 is a hundred-mile race. So, what's that, like over three days or something?

"Actually Brian, my finishing time was just under nineteen hours."

"Bull****! I mean, c'mon, you're kidding, right?"

"No Brian, that was my time. Check your notes."

"Wow, I never knew such a thing existed, so these guys today—"

"And girls, Brian."

"Um, right, so these guys AND girls today are trying to run a hundred kilometres through the French Alps; sheesh, that's gotta be tough!"

"That's a hundred miles, Brian."

"Bull****, my notes say a hundred…miles—oh!"

"Yes Brian, a hundred miles, in probably about fifteen hours, and many of the medal favourites are women."

"Wow, I never knew such a thing existed. So men AND women in the same race, with no gender categories and even odds at winning? That's awesome! So, why is that, Ailsa?"

"Several reasons, Brian, perhaps the most important being that running long distances is as much about mental strength as it is physical strength. Success comes from a commitment to process rather than results, and in a long race, intelligent processing of all the factors naturally breeds results.

It may also be due to the fact that success in a long race is largely attributed to training for injury prevention—you can run a lot farther, and a lot faster, on a healthy leg than you can on one with a strained IT band— so effective training has no gender bias.

I can't explain it completely, Brian, but there is no disputing the data: when running distances gets longer, women get better."

"All right, so here we are, waiting for the leaders to drop down off the final summit of Mont Blanc. And here he comes—I mean here she comes —check that, here THEY come."

"It's Kilian and Emilie, Brian. They are both world-beaters on the ultrarunning stage, and they are married—to each other!"

"Ok, this just keeps getting better. How does the world not know about this sport? It's simply fascinating!"

"And they're getting closer—only 500 metres to go in a hundred-mile race. Wait, it looks like Kilian is covered in mud; what's that all about, Ailsa?"

"Well Brian, mountain races almost always experience periods of bad weather, and rain-soaked trails become mud baths for the runners. You'll never see a clean finisher, Brian."

"And look, it appears that Emilie has also found the mud."

"No Brian, that's actually blood."

"What, attacked by a swarm of mosquitoes or flies, or something?"

"Nope, likely just fell a few times on the downhills. Probably cut open her knees and elbows, and then wiped her face with her bloody hands—no problem, happens all the time. You don't even want to know what else can happen during these long races, Brian, but it's probably the kind of thing you can't say on TV."

"It's Kilian and Emilie, side by side. Spouses, competing for an Olympic gold medal side by side—really? This has got to be the greatest thing EVER!"

"And at the finish, it's Emilie taking the gold, and Kilian the silver. Oh my, this is too good, pinch me and wake me up."

"Pinch me and wake me up."

"Pinch me and wake me up."

I truly believe that this will not remain just a dream for much longer!

***

BACK TO MY RACE AT LEADVILLE. As I descended down Hope Pass for the final time, I started to feel an intense pain in my feet that was much different than I had ever experienced ever before. A couple of miles before meeting up with Sharon at the sixty-mile aid station, I crossed a river, saturating my shoes and socks, when suddenly it felt like nails were being forced up through the arches of my feet.

It was now completely dark on the trail but the aid station ahead was brightly illuminated, with dozens of people lining the course waiting for their runners to arrive. As I stumbled into the aid station, I collapsed into Sharon's arms, barely able to walk.

"I will not commit, I will quit."

I now had to face the reality of accepting my first "Did Not Finish" (DNF), and I felt completely devastated.

"I am weaker than I thought I was…and I did less than I thought I would!"

The only respite from this truly demoralizing and punishing defeat came an hour or so later, as Sharon guided me slowly and painfully back to our hotel room. The prospect of pulling my shoes off my swollen and battered feet was daunting, but somehow Sharon managed to gently ease them off. As she rolled back my soiled socks, Sharon gasped at the sight she was facing: the pale thin layer of macerated outer skin was literally peeling off the bottom of my feet, exposing the raw and damaged deep tissue below. Trench Foot!

Over the next thirty minutes, Sharon tenderly washed my feet with warm soapy water, then lightly guided her fingers around the periphery of the damage. The nerves in my feet had been so overly stimulated during the race that every neuron was in an ultra-heightened state, and the sensation of touch was now regenerating my entirely broken-down body and mind. I could imagine this complete and acute awareness of my nervous system might be like an LSD-fuelled night at a Grateful Dead concert!

LEADVILLE organizers, AND IN PARTICULAR, Ken Chlouber, are somewhat famous in running circles for their almost evangelical approach to inspiring runners. In addition to the "wise" words mentioned earlier, Ken tosses out a further credo in his pre-race motivational speech:

"Yeah, it's gonna hurt, but it will only hurt for thirty hours. But if you quit, well, that hurt's gonna last a lifetime!"

I STILL hurt.

Spectators line the sides of Boylston Street as runners make their way to the finish at the Boston Marathon. I met Sharon as she stood under the black Lenox Hotel sign visible about halfway up the left side of the photo.

Running in my first Chicago Marathon, 2011.

Sharon and I standing at the top of Hope Pass, the highest point in the Leadville Trail 100 race route.

Waiting at 4:00 a.m. in downtown Leadville, Colorado for the start of the Leadville Trail 100 race.

Running through dry trails (right), and wet trails (below), in the Sinister 7 100-mile trail run.

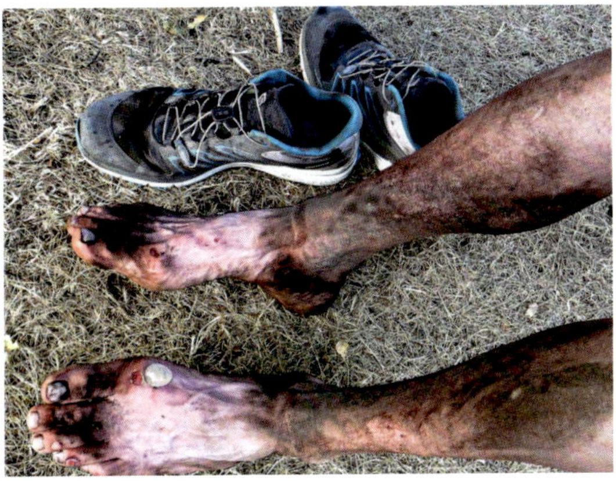

Constant reminders of our grizzly friends on the trail at Sinister 7 (above).

The battered state of my feet, as I presented them to the medics at the Sinister 7 aid station.

Running along the trails in the Leadville Trail 100 (above left), and Sinister 7 (top right and below). (Sinister 7 credit: Raven Eye Photography)

Clark and Brad's "Field of Dreams": the McNabb Valley Moto Park in Minnedosa, Manitoba. (credit: Jason Moore)

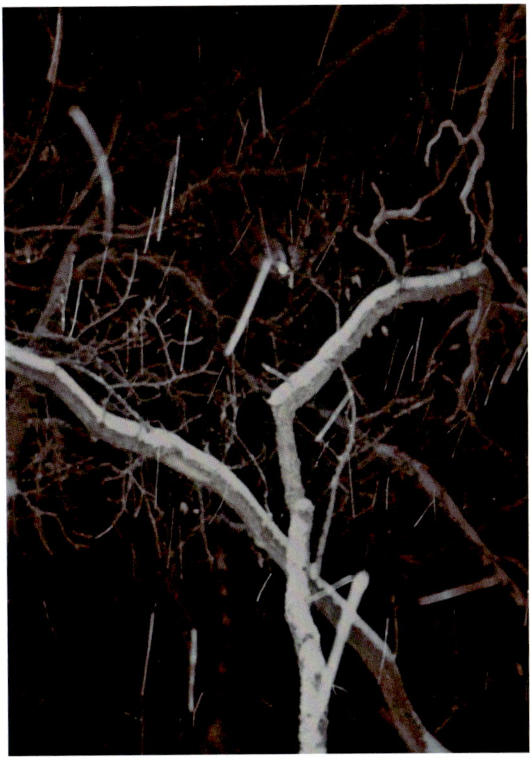

A winter night with the coyotes in the Brandon Hills.

The Leadville llamas and the Hopeless aid station (above and right).

The energy and excitement of an ultra marathon aid station (left and below). These photos were taken at the Twin Lakes aid station near Leadville.

Six

Seven Sins

As disappointed as I was at pulling out of Leadville, I have come to learn that DNFs in long races are more the norm than the exception: it is not uncommon for 70% of runners to not finish in any given race. Since Leadville, I have suffered through a few more unfortunate non-finishes, most notably twice at the notorious Sinister 7 race in the Alberta Rockies, as well as the ridiculously brutal Actif Epica race in Manitoba.

My second DNF at Sinister 7 can again be attributed partly to physical pain, as my bruised, bloodied, and blistered feet once again sabotaged my race. After a fairly comfortable start at a good pace, I eventually pulled into the third aid station, about eight hours into the race, and immediately took refuge in the medical tent, where I pulled off my shoes and socks and presented my disgustingly battered feet to a very caring—yet clearly amateur—crew of "medics."

As is typical with my feet on long races, the toenails had continuously been pounded on the downhills, resulting in swelling and a bulbous and bloody mess in the nail beds. Normally I would wait until my race was finished and then hide away in the bush or a bathroom or my daughter's deck and pick away at the offending nails with the hope of relieving the pressure. However, at this point in the race I was generally feeling pretty good, so I thought I would take a bit of time now and get the pressure relieved, so I could try to finish the race without constant pain.

It turned out to be quite a comical scene in the tent, as a small group of "nurses" took turns trying to figure out what to do with my ghastly phalanges. Sharon brought me a can of Orange Crush and a turkey sandwich, and I casually and comfortably leaned back in a chair eating my lunch while watching a young woman (who appeared to be maybe twenty years old) pull on some latex gloves, wipe my toes with alcohol, and delicately insert the needle of a syringe into the bulging nail bed trying to extract the blood.

As I enjoyed a second sandwich, I couldn't help but wince at every cautious insertion, waiting for the needle to pierce an already overly stimulated nerve in the base of my toe, which would inevitably jolt me out of the chair in wild screams of pain.

After fifteen minutes of prodding and piercing, my sweet attendant managed to avoid piercing a nerve, but also failed to withdraw any substantial blood or relieve any pressure; in defeat, she handed the needle off to a second and then a third attendant to finish the procedure.

These ongoing frustrations and failures finally drew the attention of a more elderly aide, whom I assumed to be "qualified" but just as easily could have been a volunteer from the jellybean table. At any rate, she approached my injuries with an odd air of amazement and confidence.

Sharon handed me a large jar of fruit cocktail, which I ate while leaning forward in my own combination of awe and angst, watching the procedure unfold in front of me. The new/old recruit grabbed my feet with her (ungloved) hands, and as sweet syrup from the fruit cocktail ran down my face, she proceeded to squeeze and prod and prick my toes, releasing a complementary stream of blood and plasma which covered her bare hands and dripped down on her feet below. "Oh My!" she exclaimed as the various juices flowed freely, "There we go!"

She then doused my feet with what looked like a homemade reagent of mercury and iodine, bandaged me up to the point that my toes would barely squeeze into my shoes, and sent me back out to the mountain. Over the next four hours, my feet held up rather well and my physical state was not the worst it has ever been, so my decision to pull out of the race at the next checkpoint was largely the result of mental exhaustion. After about twelve hours and ninety kilometres, I just could not tolerate the thought of basically walking for another fifteen hours through the mountains at night. So I surrendered.

AT THAT POINT, MY MIND was constantly dragging me back to the pain of my inaugural Sinister 7, where the physical and psychological struggles were more severe. I went into that event feeling strong and confident, and for the first eight hours I was running and climbing at a steady pace—a pace I felt I could keep up and continue for another fifteen hours to finish the race.

Things began to change in that first race once I headed into the third section of the course. Leg Three of Sinister 7 is, in fact, quite sinister indeed! It covers thirty-four kilometres of the highest and most exposed elevation in the race, with—at least in this first experience of mine—most of the trail meandering through the charred remains of a recent forest fire. Leg Three takes about six hours to finish and exposes runners to the intense midday sun for the entire route.

In most years, the highest proportion of the runners who drop out of the race do so after Leg Three; it just sucks the life completely out of you!

Because of the unshaded nature of the route, a big part of the challenge of Leg Three is staying hydrated. Dehydration is the most real and dangerous affliction one can suffer during midday exposed runs, and on that day the danger was very real. As much as I would try to drink enough water and electrolytes, I just couldn't seem to get enough fluid into me.

I needed to look no further than straight down to realize I was quickly approaching the point of no return. On most trail runs, I can pee pretty much every hour, but now, about four hours into Leg Three, I was stopping for my first pee since the last aid station. Every trail runner knows the sign of impending dehydration and heatstroke, and I now had it: urine the colour and consistency of butterscotch pudding!

Luckily, about five hours into the leg, I came across a small rivulet flowing down the mountain wall, where I was able to fill up with a gallon of revitalizing ice-cold mountain run-off while laying my body down so water could flow over me from head to toe. This respite from the heat reinvigorated me and I was able to run the remaining few kilometres of the leg to the next aid station, where Sharon was waiting for me with enough food and drink for a small family reunion.

One of the most perplexing and disappointing parts of a long race, however, is the complete loss of one's appetite. Prior to the race, Sharon and I had loaded up the cooler with pizza, ham and cheese sandwiches, apple pastries, banana loaf, chocolate bars, and pop. But once I was presented with this feast, I could hardly tolerate even a sniff of food.

As hard as you try to train your mind to anticipate this hunger-free state and gather everything you can think of that might stimulate your tastebuds, when hunger is suppressed by heat and fatigue eating is just not possible. One notable exception occurred in the middle of the night during my only successful completion of a hundred-miler (the Spruce Woods Ultra near my hometown) where I reluctantly ate a bite of grilled cheese sandwich (gross, at the time, I thought) and then proceeded to sit in a warming tent for a full hour as volunteers cooked me up an additional four sandwiches: I couldn't seem to get enough of them. It was delightful!

But in the midst of Sinister 7, I was only able to force down a couple of fuel gels, chased by lots of water and pop. Sharon was worried that my lack of calories was going to be an issue as I slowly made my way up the mountain to embark on the next leg of the race, but my empty stomach and I pressed on, regardless.

By all accounts Leg Four is not nearly as challenging as Leg Three. It is about ten kilometres shorter, passes through a canopy of trees through much of the route, and is run during the cooler part of the late afternoon and early evening. In addition, I had completed a training run on this leg a few days earlier, so I was actually feeling pretty confident as I started.

Then the skies opened up!

When approaching the end of Leg Three, I had noticed dark storm clouds accumulating over the mountains in the direction of Leg Four. I knew there was a good chance I would be getting very wet very soon, but I threw on a light rain jacket and, as I left Sharon, confidently turned and yelled to her that I would see her in about four hours.

The first thirty minutes or so of rain were actually very rejuvenating; the cool water on my face and the drop in temperature was therapeutic. But then the rain intensified, the temperature plunged, and lightning surrounded me. The trails now filled with water and mud and running became challenging as the lugs on the soles of my shoes held on to the mud like rebar in concrete. I quickly became saturated and a relentless chill made its way into the core of my body. As well, the constant lightning and thunder was becoming frightening!

As miserable as I was starting to feel, I was able to find some comfort and a bit of levity in the complete resurgence of my urinary system. Lots of water at the previous aid station and the cool temperatures now allowed my system to process and excrete urine like I had never thought possible. The urge to take a leak was becoming so frequent that I was finding it both challenging and time-consuming to jump off the trail, scoot behind a tree, drop my shorts, and waste twenty seconds waiting for my bladder to empty. Every time I would stop to pee a trailing runner would pass me, and I was getting a bit "pissy" about falling behind.

So, I simply stopped "stopping" and instead just peed as I ran! The first time was difficult, as grown men generally do not choose to pee their pants, but once I was able to release the natural inhibition, nature took over. I found myself almost gleeful, soaking my shorts as I ran and feeling the warm fluid flow down my legs and into my shoes. It was quite liberating.

I didn't even care that at one point a woman was running only a few yards behind me; the rain was coming down so hard that my shorts, legs, and shoes were constantly going through a new rinse cycle, so I was the only one who would have noticed what I was doing, anyway. Heck, in those conditions, she may have been doing the same thing—the trail is the toilet for everyone! If you've ever seen the movie *Dirty Rotten Scoundrels,* you'd have recognized my face reflecting Steve Martin's expression as his goofy character Ruprecht—surrounded by pretentious guests— quietly lets it flow under the dinner table!

Shits and giggles can only last so long in conditions like that, and soon I found my body was starting to seize up in the cold, my soaking feet were developing painful blisters (as usual), and my mental resolve was weakening fast.

The rain continued for the entire leg, and by the time I arrived at the next aid station, Sharon had been waiting for me at least two hours longer than expected. I stumbled into Aid Station Four, and was greeted by a scene that could have been mistaken for the front lines of the Western Front in WWI.

The ground was a complete mud bath as rain continued to pour down, and fallen runners were comforted by their support crews, with more than a few competitors making their way to the medic tent. There was only one other small tent that could provide shelter for perhaps ten people, and it was full, so Sharon tended to me out in open, trying to keep me warm with extra jackets and a soggy blanket. We didn't even have a chair for me to sit on as my sweet, lovely, and equally cold and soaked support crew recounted her tale of attempts to carry all the gear from our car to this aid station. Her afternoon, as it turned out, had not been much better than mine.

Upon leaving the previous aid station (where I'd been unable to eat), Sharon began to pack up her gear in the rain in preparation for the journey to meet me at Aid Station Four. When she had opened the cooler to load up some remaining drinks, she'd noticed that the bag of ice—which had been in the cooler since early that morning—had melted, and that all my food was soaking in the water.

Even though I had left Sharon after eating very little and having no interest in the food we had packed, she knew she couldn't arrive at the next aid station with nothing but soggy sandwiches. So, on her way to our next meeting point, Sharon frantically darted into the local grocery store to re-load everything that had been wasted, and then proceeded to the aid station, hoping to see me in a couple of hours.

Aid Station Four was located several miles out of town on a small plateau above a highway tourist stop. Prior to the start of the race, organizers had informed support crews that they could pull up to the bottom of the hill at the base of the plateau, where they could then unload supplies and race officials would then transport everything to the aid station up the hill. However, when Sharon arrived, she was told that crews would need to park a few hundred metres away and haul everything they would need up the hill themselves. The rain was still falling hard as Sharon filled her arms with everything she could possibly carry, simultaneously struggling to pull our giant cooler through the mud up a steep hill—while wearing just beach sandals.

As Sharon later described the ridiculous situation she was in, I had to laugh at how pathetic the two of us were on that day. When she finally arrived at the plateau, she was forced to unload everything on the ground in a slough of mud and, with no shelter available, simply stand in the mud waiting for my arrival.

When I finally arrived, much later than anticipated, both of us were miserably cold, wet, and covered in mud; still, we proceeded to work through the aid station checklist as planned. After all her trouble and efforts to replenish the food and haul the cooler up the muddy slopes, I felt terrible when I was unable to tolerate even one bite of sandwich or anything else she had brought for me.

After we'd been standing and shivering in the rain for ten minutes, another crew offered us one of their chairs inside the small tent, so we squeezed into a tiny corner of dry ground under this canopy. Volunteers at this aid station had large pots of meatballs and scalloped potatoes cooking, which stimulated my hunger a bit, so Sharon spent the next ten or fifteen minutes bringing me some much-needed hot food.

With calories in my belly, the remaining concern was the wet and near-hypothermic state I was in. After trying to warm up under the toy-sized tent with wind and rain blowing into our bodies and faces, we eventually gave up and sought out professional help. After we made our way to the medic tent, I was immediately wrapped in thermal blankets and fed hot broth.

The medics here were noticeably concerned—and a bit annoyed—that we didn't have any dry clothes with us. In my preparation, I had brought a rain jacket with me but had packed away the rest of my warm clothing in a drop bag which was waiting for me at the next aid station. I had known I would need extra clothing for the six-hour overnight leg that followed that aid station, but never thought I would need it at this point in the race.

After much debate in my mind about either continuing with the race or stopping, I decided to head back out on the course, hoping that running would eventually bring my core temperature back up. With that decision made, I reluctantly crawled out from under the cozy blanket, bade farewell to Sharon, and headed out on Leg Five.

For the first half-hour of Leg Five my legs and back were as rigid as trekking poles and my body shook in spasms as it desperately tried to elevate my internal temperature. This uncontrollable shaking eventually faded, and before long I was running comfortably once more.

Within an hour, I found myself with a small group of other runners who themselves were suffering from various states of physical and mental dysfunction; together we headed up into a thickly wooded mountain ascent just as dark was approaching. The scene here would be one that producers of horror movies would salivate over: the night had become blacker than black, the narrow trail wound its way through thick forest, the ground was saturated and had become one continuous channel of water and mud traversing the entire route, and the cold thick mist from the day's rain engulfed everything.

It was beyond eerie, as all of us were too tired and miserable to talk and the mountain was completely quiet. The reflection of light from our headlamps in the mist limited our visibility to no more than a few metres directly ahead, making it feel like the trees on either side were creeping closer inch by inch until they were on top of us.

The mountain was very steep, and not being able to see much of the trail ahead made it feel like we were climbing to the moon. Add to this the fact that this section of the Rocky Mountains is heavily populated with cougars and grizzly bears, and choosing to be here of our own free will seemed a ludicrous decision. It would have been a ludicrous decision even if we'd been experienced backcountry hikers, which we weren't.

When we eventually arrived at a checkpoint halfway through Leg Five, we were informed that in fact both cougars and grizzly bears were on the course with us that night! One group of runners had to be pulled off the course while race organizers shooed the bear off the trail; a second group had to huddle together while throwing rocks at a cougar that was stalking them along the way.

PERHAPS THE STRANGEST PART of this very strange endeavour is that during these bizarre, scary, and sometimes dangerous moments on the trail, I rarely experienced any real fear.

That's true of all my races. After enduring hours of mental and physical stress, all I ever think about is finishing, and that thought is all my weakened mind has room for. While running at home, however, a healthy respect for the unknown (and perhaps a little bit of fear) acts like the perfect seasoning in a great meal; it just raises the experience to a whole new level.

One of my favourite running experiences at home is strapping on my snowshoes and heading out to the forested trails on a cold and dark winter night. I almost always find myself completely alone, running slowly through the night with my headlamp guiding the way.

The dry, cold Manitoba air provides amazing acoustics as my shoes skim across the surface of the snow with a pleasing swoosh-swoosh sound, a sound that's harmonically balanced by the gentle crunch-crunch as my cleats bite into the crust of that surface. This winter symphony is completed by the intermittent sounds of winter wildlife: the hoot of an owl above me, the breaking of branches as a deer gracefully bounds through the trees beside me, and the distant and not-so-distant howls of coyotes that seem to completely surround me.

It is this constant howling that adds an element of awareness to my winter runs. When I'm out alone on these nights, I keep reminding myself, with a degree of uneasy uncertainty, that coyotes typically have no interest in attacking or eating humans. However, when I round a corner and see the reflection of my headlamp off a coyote's eyes farther ahead on the trail, I can't help but wonder if this one will go rogue!

Moments later, as my light catches the fleeting glimpse of a second coyote darting across the trail and disappearing into the woods, my mind flips back to similar scenes from movies or passages from books: moments where packs of wolves stealthily stalk lost and unsuspecting hikers.

Of course, after years of choosing to run in these conditions, real fear does not follow me into the woods, but I have to admit there are nights on the trail where, when the howling begins, I find myself practicing jabbing my trekking pole into the darkness—just in case I need to "poke" a beast as it creeps up from behind me!

***

AN INTERESTING AND SOMETIMES FRUSTRATING feature of Sinister 7 is that it can be run as a solo event or a team event, with different team members running different legs of the race. In the first couple of legs, this blend of runners serves as motivation for the solo runners, as they adjust their pace relative to the generally faster relay runners. However, as the race drags on into the night, the presence of faster team runners becomes a bit of an annoyance.

As much as I try to be happy for these runners, their presence does start to wear on me after a while. While I'm dragging my soiled and broken body through the night after fifteen hours on the trail, relay runners, having just started their race only an hour earlier, come zipping past from behind, all clean and perky. I really am happy for them, as they are clearly enjoying their experience on the trail, yet somehow it just burns me to be on the same trail at the same time as them, with only one of us suffering.

About half-way through Leg Five of my first Sinister 7, one of these relay runners approached us from behind, merrily whistling away as he slowed while passing us. Again, I feel terrible for harbouring any negative thoughts about this person; after all, he was just like me, a guy out running trails for the sheer joy and challenge of the experience. It's just that when you're feeling completely beat up by the mountain and pain latches on to every breath and step, being lapped by some pain-free "Pollyanna" becomes a bit demoralizing.

On this night, the relay runner in question was overly bouncy and cheerful as he passed us, wishing us luck (as if luck had anything to do with anything at this point of the race), but I then noticed, as he started to run ahead of us, that his headlamp was very dim.

Over the years, I have invested in several high-end lights and have come to appreciate how important illumination is on the trail. On this part of the trail, the conditions were very technical—heavy rains had carved continuous ravines through the mud and the ground was covered in loose rocks—and the night was very dark, so his lack of preparation definitely registered with me. No more than a few minutes later, after cresting a small hill and slowly making our way down a steep decline on the other side, we noticed the relay runner's light disappear momentarily, followed by the light dancing from air to ground to trees as the runner tumbled down the hill, screaming as his previously clean, fresh, and pain-free body pounded into the rocks.

The three of us quickly scrambled down the trail to assess the damage and help our fallen comrade. The cumulative illumination of our lights revealed scrapes, blood, and mud, but no obvious serious injuries. After consoling the relay runner for a few minutes, we wished *him* luck for the rest of his race, as he remained tending to his wounds and we slowly limped towards the next checkpoint. Within minutes the three of us "dead men walking" became four, as the bloodied relay runner joined us and quietly stuck by our sides the rest of the way. Misery really does love company!

As we finally approached the lights of the next aid station, I knew my race was finished. Yet oddly enough, when I ultimately met Sharon I wasn't overcome with feelings of failure or despair; I simply accepted that on this day I was beaten by the weather and the mountains and that I would lick my wounds and continue on, more determined than ever to keep training and pushing myself to try and discover the limits of my abilities. Defeat felt both liberating and empowering.

Seven

Eyes Frozen Shut

If ultrarunning races were to be placed on a continuum with Leadville and Sinister 7 at one end, then surely Actif Epica would sit at the extreme opposite. Summer mountain running, characterized by high altitude, extreme heat, biblical rains, technical terrain, and wild beasts, contrasts sharply with the flat prairies, bitter cold and wind, snow-covered trails, and the near-complete absence of other lifeforms that runners encounter at Actif Epica.

Actif Epica is a 125-kilometre race run in February across the prairies of southeastern Manitoba. In some years, a Manitoba February can bring spring-like conditions with melting temperatures, calm winds, and blue skies. But what is more likely, and what I encountered in the days leading up to my attempt to run Actif Epica, are dangerously cold temperatures with equally dangerous winds. Event organizers had even adopted a safety guideline that would cancel the race if the projected windchill on race day was to remain at -40° C or lower throughout the race, and as I made my way at 4:00 a.m. to a bus that would transport us to the start line 125 kilometres south of downtown Winnipeg, the wind chill was -43° C. But forecasters predicted a slight drop in wind would occur, thus warming the perceived temperature by a few degrees. The race was on.

IN ADDITION TO my normal winter training leading up to the race, I felt I needed to experience training in actual race conditions, so I enlisted help from my friend Clark. Clark is a farmer outside of my hometown and among many of his admirable qualities is an almost self-sacrificing dedication to helping others. I approached Clark about coming to his farm on an upcoming evening and using his garage as a staging area for an overnight practice run around his and several other neighbouring farmyards, and he happily obliged.

I wanted to experience what it would be like to spend an entire night in cold, darkness, and isolation. When I explained to Clark that the race route would be split between country roads and trails across fields (which I would manoeuvre by strapping on snowshoes if deep snow was encountered), he offered to take his tractor and plow through his snow-covered canola fields, carving me a trail across his property. So out he went, on the day before my arrival, to create his own little "Field of Dreams" for me.

IN ALL SERIOUSNESS, Clark really has created his own legitimate Field of Dreams in the form of a world-class motocross track no more than twenty-five metres from his house. Clark and his son Brad have committed many years of their lives to the construction of this track, so that his now adrenalin-fuelled grandkids would have a professional arena to develop their skills.

The commitment of Clark and Brad to this track, the McNabb Valley Moto Park, as it is known, has attracted interest from across Canada; several prestigious races are now held there every year, including races from the National circuit which draws the best professional riders from across North America.

It is quite an amazing scene to watch the way this place is transformed, from a dirt track and a couple of empty fields to a small city of hundreds of fans and dozens of professional crews sporting some of the largest and most colourful rigs I have ever seen. In the days leading up to the Canadian Nationals race, sponsored riders from such big names as Honda, Kawasaki, and KTM begin arriving at Clark's farm, hauling bright, polished, chrome-covered semi-trailer trucks carrying multiple bikes, along with technical crews, nutritionists, therapists, and a variety of other services for the professional riders.

A race of this stature also draws affiliated sponsors, ranging from energy drinks to engine oil, who surround the track with colourful logos promoting their products, and media outlets who set up film crews to broadcast the race on national television. Come race day, with fifty or more finely tuned bikes screaming at redline rpm's, Clark's small family farm could be mistaken for a Saturday afternoon at Daytona Speedway!

An event of this scale requires a co-ordinated effort from many people, so I gladly volunteered to help Clark and Brad prepare the track and grounds prior to the event, and to help out during the race. And as it turned out, race day actually provided me with a unique training session for my own upcoming races.

Clark hosted the Motocross Nationals in early June, and my next race —my second attempt at Sinister 7—was to be held just three weeks later. As I would be giving up critical training time to spend the day at the race, I decided to make the most of the situation and arrive at Clark's dressed in full running gear, hoping to run a few laps around the farm.

My uniform for the day included shorts and a singlet, bright red bug-eyed glasses that would be just as fitting on a 1970's punk-rocker, a Canadian flag the size of a tea towel tucked under my cap and hanging down the back of my neck (to provide protection from the sun), and a pair of FiveFingers toe shoes on my feet—making me look like some sort of forest creature from a child's fantasy movie!

Once the gates opened for the day, the grounds filled with hundreds of hard-core motocross fans sporting trucker hats and Red Bull T-shirts. Mud-covered riders wearing full race armour navigated their bikes through the crowd, heading to their crew stations for maintenance between races. Bookending all of this were the Rock Star promotional girls dressed in painted-on spandex; they mingled with the crowd, distributing caffeine-loaded energy drinks while Clark, Brad, and their cadre of helpers patrolled the grounds in a convoy of pick-ups, large water trucks, and ATVs. The grounds were oozing with testosterone, and in my trail running garb I looked just a bit out of place!

With professional co-ordination and execution, the race progressed flawlessly; my contribution to the event was simply to wander around looking for ways to help out. The event was spread out over a large area, so I took the opportunity to run everywhere I went. I alternated from sprints around the perimeter of the track picking up garbage, to running to Clark's shop to grab a drill for a racer and his crew, to jogging out to the nearby slough where I helped pump water into the trucks used to maintain the track between races.

Periodically, I headed over to the entry gates where I helped guide cars to parking spots around the farm. It was challenging and time-consuming trying to convey directions to drivers, so ultimately I simply got the cars to follow me as I ran ahead through the canola fields to parking areas. I would get to the top of a hill, point in the direction of the field for a car to head towards, then turn around and run back to the gates to do it all again.

During one of these circuits, Clark's wife Sherri told me that the outdoor toilet set up at the entrance was out of toilet paper. Since I would be running past a second toilet further up the grounds, I offered to stop in there on the way back and grab a roll to bring back with me. When I poked my head into this second commode, I noticed that it was also "TP-free." I quickly headed back to the gate, where I told Sherri that I would need to locate a third toilet on the other side of the racetrack and check if it had any paper.

Running through the maze of rigs and fans, I was able to locate the third outhouse which, of course, also had no toilet paper. I then ran around to the perimeter of the track to where Brad was stationed watching the race. He informed me that a supply of toilet paper was stored in his friend's black truck parked near Clark's house. I ran back to the house where I spotted a black truck…with NO toilet paper.

Clark's neighbour Max was at the end of the lane guiding traffic to the entrance farther down the road, so I ran down to him to see if he knew which truck I was looking for. He pointed to a truck sitting in the ditch across the road, where I was finally able to locate the toilet paper. I grabbed about ten rolls and sprinted down the road towards the gate.

As cars were following me, I can't help but wonder what they thought they were actually witnessing in front of them: some strange mutant hybrid of a Hobbit crossed with the front-man from the Ramones, sporting a superhero cape while clutching a bag of Charmin and moving as if he were chasing Usain Bolt in a hundred-metre dash!

I spent the better part of the afternoon scurrying around the track and grounds, moving from toilet to toilet, feeling an odd sense of pride in keeping the facilities functional for the remainder of the day. I never did see the entire television broadcast of the race, but sometimes I wonder if, on close inspection, TSN actually got a passing shot of this strange toilet paper courier!

***

BACK TO FEBRUARY, on Clark's farm, and my preparations for Actif Epica. After clearing snow for about 500 metres, the front end of Clark's tractor suddenly sank. He had unknowingly cleared a path right into a slough and his tractor was now perched nose-down over a ten-foot drop, unable to move in any direction. Clark's cousin Barry, who farms a few miles away, was incredulous when he arrived with his much larger tractor to extract the sunken snowplow:

"What the hell are you doing?"

"Plowing my field."

"It's February!"

"It's for Mark."

"What?"

"Yeah, it's for Mark, I'm plowing a path for him so he can practice running and snowshoeing through the fields overnight."

"What?"

"Yeah, it's for Mark, he's running a thirty-hour race across the open fields south of Winnipeg next weekend."

"What?!"

And so it went. Clark eventually cleared my path and the next night I arrived at midnight to run around the frozen fields at -30° C. I don't think anyone in the area really believed in my sanity—or Clark's, for that matter. Clark's mother Marion at least accepted that I really would be out in the wild overnight, so she made sure to leave a light on in her farmyard and left her doors open in case I either came to my senses or was near freezing to death and needed a place to warm up.

As the night progressed, every time I would round the bend that approached her lane I would glance up to Marion's place, hoping not to see her sweet face peeking out through the frost of her window watching out for me! I didn't want to worry her and keep her awake.

The night turned out to be a successful training run and now, whenever we see each other, Clark and I have a laugh as he talks about feeling guilty for sitting on his couch most of the night, wrapped in a blanket with a Dagwood sandwich in his hands, following my headlamp as it went bobbing past his house every hour!

AMONG ULTRA-RACES, ACTIF EPICA is both unusual and cruel. The course is completely unmarked, requiring runners to carry a map, course cues, and a GPS for navigation. In addition, the race is almost completely self-supported, meaning that aside from some relief in halls or arenas in the few small towns along the route, racers must carry two litres of water, food for the entire day, and all extra clothing and miscellaneous gear. Into my backpack I stuffed two winter jackets, snow pants, two extra pairs of gloves and mittens, changes of socks, shirts and long underwear, sunglasses and ski goggles, an emergency space blanket, a strip of magnesium from my chemistry lab in case I needed an intense source of ignition for a fire, half a dozen hot packs for frozen hands and feet, snowshoes and poles, a couple of cans of coconut water, a few chocolate bars and sandwiches, and some nuts and raisins. Oh, and a pound of butter!

A non-negotiable safety rule for this race is that for an official finish to be recorded, three conditions must be met: runners must complete the race in under thirty hours, runners must cross the finish line with all the gear they started the day with, and runners must carry at least two thousand calories of food across the finish line. Race veterans have determined that the most easily measured and compressed dose of at least a couple thousand calories is a pound of butter; hence, stuffing a few sticks of frozen fat in the bottom of a pack has become the standard gear for most runners.

Despite the extreme weather, my body never really suffered from the cold. Proper clothing, hydration and nutrition, along with constant motion, kept the cold from penetrating my core or freezing my hands or feet. My eyes, on the other hand, were a completely different story.

In order to read the maps and GPS, I needed to wear prescription sunglasses throughout the day, and to prevent frostbite to my face, I also needed to wear a balaclava. Within the first thirty minutes of the start, and throughout the rest of the day, the cold air and constant north wind in my face caused my balaclava to freeze solid and my sunglasses to freeze up with frost from my breath. The frozen fabric around my face simply reflected each breath back up to my eyes, so frozen lenses made navigation challenging. I tried placing my ski goggles over my glasses, but the foam seal also froze solid and before long, the goggles became nothing more than an annoyance, so they were removed, along with my sunglasses.

At the forty-kilometre point of the race I joined two other runners, Jon and Sue, and we engaged in friendly chatter despite the punishing conditions. As it turned out, chatter became our worst enemy, as none of us were paying close enough attention to the maps: we all missed a turn on the route, leading us on a ten- kilometre extension to the race.

By the time we realized our error and returned to the route, we had added about two hours to our time in the cold and wind, and our spirits sank. By this time in the late afternoon, my eyes had reached the point of potentially serious and harmful exposure to the bright sun, cold, and wind, and I was finding it difficult to even keep them open. I would close my eyes for moments at a time, but soon my eyelids would freeze shut, and opening them became a painful and distressing challenge.

Ultimately, I resorted to pulling my toque down over my eyes and tilting my head so I could just see the heels of Jon and Sue in front of me. This rather feeble attempt to keep on going finally brought us all to the halfway point in the race, where runners were allowed to take refuge in a small-town arena while volunteers served them up platefuls of hot perogies.

As my eyes melted and I began preparing for a return to the course, I decided to take a few minutes to dry my balaclava, shirt, and mittens under a hot air dryer in the washroom. When I returned to the arena, a medic was just finishing cutting Jon's frozen beard from his frozen jacket, while Sue was dressed and ready to head out on the trail.

Sue was anxious to get going, as our departure from the route earlier would make it difficult to finish the race under the thirty-hour cut-off. This was of particular significance to Sue, as a finish in Actif Epica, along with her finishes in two previous long-distance winter races, would earn her an award called the Order of the Hrimthurs, and the accompanying elite status in the running community.

With Jon's "beardectomy" complete, he was now ready to join Sue, and the two of them returned to the course. It would take me at least an extra ten minutes to get myself ready, so I had to remain behind and contemplate my options.

It was now dark, and I was the last runner still in the race. I knew that I would have to navigate for the remaining twelve hours alone—with no light, and basically no vision, at -40° C! Thankfully, my brain was not frozen along with my eyes, and after sitting with my head in my hands for another ten minutes, I decided that continuing with this race alone, under these conditions, would be extremely dangerous and highly irresponsible. Once again, I accepted defeat and headed home. Sorry, Clark!

Eight

Laz's Laps

In long-distance trail running, nothing drains horsepower from a runner's engine like hills and heat. But during the inaugural Outrun Rare Backyard Ultra in Alberta in 2019, mud knocked both gravity and the sun off the punishment podium in epic fashion.

The Outrun Rare Backyard Ultra is fashioned after the original Backyard Ultra in Tennessee, whose race director is none other than Lazarus Lake, the same race director of the notorious Barkley Marathons. Laz's race in Tennessee, called Big's Backyard Ultra (named after his dog Big), is quickly becoming just as popular and menacing as its more famous big brother.

A backyard ultra is quite simply a race with no end! Runners must complete a 6.71-kilometre lap in one hour, and then continue completing laps on the hour until only one runner remains in the game. This "last runner standing" competition can yield some almost unbelievable results, as witnessed by Laz's 2018 race. In this race, the last two runners on the course competed against each other until their sixty-seventh lap, until ultimately one runner succumbed to exhaustion, leaving the final competitor to complete one last lap for a total accumulated time of almost sixty-eight hours and a distance of over 450 kilometres! All of this while stopping and resting for no more than a few minutes each hour.

To be honest, a race that repeats loops over and over again is about as appealing to me as walking to the grocery store fifty times. However, over the last few years (thanks to Laz's magnetic personality), backyard ultras are popping up all over the world, attracting a diverse range of runners seeking coveted entries to the unofficial "World Championship" in Tennessee each October.

As much as my impatient personality can't stand repetition, I too was drawn into this peculiar and somehow inspiring challenge of repeating as many boring, mind-numbing loops as possible.

At its core, a backyard ultra is not about athleticism, but rather willpower. Pretty much any Sunday jogger can run 6.71 kilometres in one hour and, given the right conditions, can likely repeat at least a half-dozen loops this long before shutting down. Now, present this challenge to a serious group of ultrarunners of varying speeds and stamina, and the prospect of actually winning a backyard race becomes a very real possibility for everyone. Bring a bunch of bodies with reasonable fitness to this race and the strongest mind takes the trophy.

So I suppose that was the attraction for me at the Outrun Rare event in 2019: an aging body that wasn't broken and an optimistic and stubborn mind that insisted victory could just as easily be mine as anyone else's. That determination persisted, unfortunately, until only about halfway through the first lap, when a thick, soggy blanket of clouds decided to drop down on top of our little 6.71-kilometre loop and squeeze out constant rain for the next ten hours.

The course was cut through a low-lying forest along the banks of a small river, before it turned onto a half-mile horse track where runners would complete one loop before heading back out to the trail. As the rain began, the soft ground on the trails turned into a channel of mud, while the horse track turned into pea soup.

I completed the first couple of laps in about forty-five minutes (pretty much what I had planned for) and was actually a bit giddy about the conditions. Oddly, it was rather fun slogging and sliding through this mud bath, knowing that within an hour I could huddle under my tarp for a few minutes, open my cooler, and eat and drink the bounty of treats I'd brought along for the ride. Then a series of whistles, (three, then two, then one) would sound the three-minute countdown, before Laz, who was with us as an honorary race director, would ring a school bell to send us back out on the course for another lap.

At about lap six, my attitude started to go from giddy to grumpy as the combination of rain and 150 runners began transforming the course from fun to foolish. It was now becoming almost impossible to run with any speed at all, and keeping one's balance in the undulating mud trough was taxing every muscle and joint in my body. The horse track was now becoming a half-mile of Hell!

With the exception of about 500 metres near the start and end of each loop, the ENTIRE course was mud, that just kept getting thicker and more tormenting with each lap. Trying to run on the horse track was punishing. I chose to run the shortest distance around the track next to the inside rail, where the slope of the ground funnelled most of the water. As the day went on, the water on this path got steadily deeper and deeper, with mud at times almost reaching my knees. Trying to run through this mess was about as strange and arduous as pretty much anywhere else I had run before. After lap seven, the race director wisely decided that the track was becoming impassable, so runners were now guided across the mud to run on the grass infield for the remainder of the race.

For the next four hours, rain and racers continued to fall, as the field quickly dropped from 150 to about forty, an attrition rate that shocked Laz and everyone else in attendance. The mud was getting so bad that it was becoming a struggle to complete the loop in under an hour. With every lap, those of us still on the course would meet the mud-caked defeated as they hung their heads in a walk of shame back to the finish. Laz would smugly hand each failed finisher a brush, where their last acknowledgement of defeat was to erase their own name from the large whiteboard hanging at the start line that displayed the names of all the runners still in contention—ownership of one's own demise to the bitter end!

During my tenth lap, I began to slow to a pace that brought me to the finish with about five minutes to spare. On lap eleven, the strain on my back and hips from the constant stride corrections in the mud reduced my last two kilometres to a turtle-paced walk; I arrived at the finish just as the three-minute whistle was sounding.

With a quick turnaround, I joined the remaining few dozen runners out on lap twelve, where I soon realized that my pace couldn't possibly bring me back to the finish in under one hour. Thus, I too hung my head and shuffled back to the finishing tent, where I was handed a brush to erase my own name from the board.

As I was gathering my gear and preparing to head home, the remaining racers and their crews began to engage in lively, optimistic chatter, as the race director announced that the river along the trail was close to breaching its banks and consequently the entire massacre of mud was being shut down. The racers were now re-routed to the horse track, where they would complete eight laps on the grass before returning to the finish. There was to be no more mud!

My heart sank as I heard this news, knowing that if I had just pushed myself through that last lap I might have found some renewed strength and optimism to continue for at least a few more hours. However, as I have learned from past races, once a DNF strikes there is always a "what if I had only…" moment, so I let it pass and headed home with a small dose of pride and large dose of excitement for my return the following year.

AN INTERESTING TWIST to the finish of this race was that to earn a coveted entry—a "golden ticket"—to the World Championship Backyard Ultra in Tennessee, Laz decreed that the last runner standing had to complete at least thirty-two laps, with no fewer than two runners completing a minimum of thirty-one laps. Laz's logic behind this and all Backyard ultras is that competition among runners must continue to the bitter end; once only one runner remains on the course, the competition is over. After twenty-five muddy laps and over one hundred miles of running, only two names, Matt and Kevin, remained on the board. Kevin appeared to be struggling to complete any further laps, while Matt still looked strong, and was most certainly destined to be the last runner standing. In a remarkable display of respect and admiration for Matt, Kevin somehow pushed his depleted body through lap thirty-one before dropping, which allowed Matt to finish lap thirty-two, thereby earning the "ticket" and the honour of joining Laz and Big in Tennessee.

AFTER YEARS OF DEDICATING my running life to the physical demands of rugged mountain races, the Backyard philosophy has now inspired me to approach every future running opportunity, whether it be training at home or racing in Bulgaria, with a new sense of emotional and psychological purpose: one where mind must always be stronger than body. I am hopeful and optimistic that this refined dedication to the sport will carry me through my sixtieth year and beyond.

Nine

The Call of Kilian

Failed finishes in ultra-running come in many different forms and for many different reasons, but none more epic than what I experienced in Tromsø, Norway. Tromsø is a small city located north of the Arctic Circle in a region as remote, rugged, and beautiful as one can imagine. I first learned of Tromsø about one year before I was to retire from a thirty-three-year teaching career. I had been navigating mountain terrain for the past seven years and my possible over-confidence and foolish nature prompted me to search for a race that would excite and challenge me like no other. If I discovered that this race existed, I would treat myself to a retirement gift and travel to it—anywhere in the world.

Enter Kilian Jornet.

Through my research on bucket-list races, I discovered that "Kilian the Great" had recently created his own epic challenge in Norway.

Considering everything that Kilian had accomplished on his climb to the top of the mountain running world, it was no surprise to me that he would only attach his name to a race worthy of his stature. The Tromsø Extreme Skyrace is part of the wildly popular Sky Running circuit throughout Europe. Sky Running, and specifically Extreme Sky Running, is a niche sport among mountain runners, in that race routes follow exposed sharp mountain ridges and steep summits with lots of elevation gain.

While its courses are not overly long by many standards—usually ranging from thirty to sixty kilometres—Extreme Sky Running presents its challenge in the danger of traversing these knife-edge ridges, and in the punishing climbs and descents. As I read race reports from past competitors and analyzed countless video clips from previous years' races at Tromsø, I was convinced that this was an event I had to experience.

Watching professional runners cautiously navigate the insanely treacherous Hamperokken ridge and then scale the near vertical wall of loose rock to a needle-point summit simultaneously made my stomach turn and heart race. More than a few race reports cautioned prospective entrants that choosing to run Tromsø should be limited to those with extreme mountain experience; the risk of falling to one's death was very real. So, with a lack of any responsible due diligence, I set my alarm and at precisely 3:00 a.m. on of the morning that registration opened, and with my hands shaking, I clicked REGISTER. Within thirty seconds of the registration page going active, there was my name, a slightly beyond-middle-aged average runner from the Canadian prairies, on the start list of one of the world's most challenging and dangerous mountain races!

PRIOR TO MAKING OUR WAY farther north to Tromsø, Sharon and I first arrived in Iceland to run through the indescribable beauty of the Laugavegur Ultra Marathon. Unless you've been to Iceland, it is difficult to put in perspective how raw, rugged, and gorgeous this place is! When travelling throughout the virtually empty countryside, we saw brilliant hues of gold, green, and purple everywhere—carpeting the varied terrain at the foot of snow-capped mountains, fading into rocky beaches and the ocean and surrounding lava fields, and framing the seemingly endless waterfalls and geothermal pools. Frequent sightings of Icelandic horses (perhaps the most adorable animal on this planet!) galloping across the landscape make you feel like you are in some kind of lost world. Sharon would often comment that the extreme and beautiful landscape is like "the birth of the earth."

The Laugavegur race follows a popular fifty-five-kilometre trail connecting primitive huts and campgrounds at either end. The trail begins in a small valley that can only be accessed by crossing a river in trucks or buses equipped with tires the size of Pluto. The huts at the starting area are surrounded by a geothermal stream generating plumes of steam that lead runners up through a steep rocky ridge that looks like it could be a breeding ground for trolls!

Once the gun sounded, I put on my game face, dialed up the compete-metre, and joined the pack of Salomon-shod Vikings. I was intent on running my best race ever. Yet, after only just a couple of kilometres, I shifted my focus. I was no longer running like a gritty trail racer pushing for the podium, but instead I started to feel more like a trekking tourist. The surrounding topography was so unique and captivating that I found myself stopping regularly to take in the grandeur of the region. It felt oddly liberating to let runner after runner pass by as I hopped off the trail to absorb the rugged beauty of Iceland—I just could not focus solely on running and let this beauty pass me by too quickly. After meandering through a series of black lava-encrusted rocky outcrops, the trail opened up to reveal a steam-filled valley floor which runners would pass through before ascending a steep slope of orange and red rock. The region was visually stunning and made me

Running through the rugged geothermal landscape at the Laugavegur Ultra Marathon in Iceland, a trail run that is as unique and spectacular as anywhere else on the planet.

Experiencing the "Ice" in Iceland as I ran across the frozen highlands in the Laugavegur Ultra Marathon.

After crossing the barren icefield, runners enter an idyllic world of lush beauty as they continue through the middle section of the Laugavegur Ultra Marathon. (Credit: Olafur Thorrisson)

Kirkjufell mountain in the Snæfellsnes Peninsula in western Iceland.

Glymur waterfall in western Iceland just outside of Reykjavik.

Hiking along part of the Hamperokken Skyrace route in northern Norway.

While talking with Kilian Jornet on the day before the Tromsø Skyrace, I still had no real sense as to the challenges I would face navigating the Hamperokken ridge and summit (seen below).

This was my first view of the beautiful, yet imposing Hamperokken ridge and summit. It was just beyond the first section of the ridge in the foreground where an American runner lost her footing and fell to the valley below.

Standing at the beginning of the Hamperokken ridge, my initial shock over this treacherous terrain had subsided, and I was actually excited and confident about turning around and moving forward towards the needle-point Hamperokken summit.

My mood had changed dramatically however, once I managed to traverse the ridge and reach the base of the Hamperokken summit. Here, Thilo and I take a break while contemplating our strategy for scaling up the near vertical wall of loose rock to the summit above.

My view after reaching the summit of Hamperokken mountain. Looking back across the ridge, Tromsdalstinden mountain is immediately beyond the ridge in the top half of the photo, while the city of Tromsø, where the race started, lies beyond the water in the very top right of the photo.

A "selfie-in -motion" while running through the lava fields in the Laugavegur Ultra Marathon.

Runners ascending the first climb in the Hamperokken Skyrace.

Looking back towards Tromsø while climbing up to the start of the Hamperokken ridge.

think that it could have served as the perfect album cover from the 70s for Boston or The Eagles!

After about ten kilometres in this Mars-like landscape, I switched back to racer mode as the trail opened up, guiding me for another ten kilometres across a wind-swept glacier. On this day, wind, sleet, and fog made progress very challenging across the partially thawed icefield. Yet, in spite of the conditions, it was quite remarkable how wonderful I felt. With ice pelting my face, I found myself laughing out loud and yelling, "Kiddi! Gummi! Ha-Ha-Ha, this is freekin' awesome!" The snow and ice that I was slogging through was bringing back memories of similar images from the Icelandic movie RAMS, in which two elderly brothers, Kiddi and Gummi, struggle for their lives while guiding their flock of sheep through the remote highlands of Iceland during a severe snowstorm.

Once out of the icefield, the Laugavegur trail crosses a few freezing cold rivers, a long windswept field of black lava dust, and then immediately drops down into a valley where I was able to run full-out into what is quite possibly the most stunning landscape I will ever see. The next several kilometres were perhaps the most memorable and most rewarding of my running life. I bounced down an undulating single-track with a cascading river to my left, steep hills carpeted in brilliant colour to my right, a single majestic mountain rising above the horizon in front, and bubbling and steaming hot pools all around me. It is truly difficult to find the words that could do justice to this scene, so one must simply try to imagine beauty in its most vivid form. This trail running experience was one that should be scooped up and sealed in a jar to be taken out and shared with anyone who is ever feeling down. Everyone, and I really do mean everyone, needs to visit Iceland once in their life!

Ten

Heaven and Hell on Hamperokken

After leaving Iceland, we arrived in Tromsø a few days before the race and spent much of our time hiking through some of the safer parts of the course. I enjoyed this time climbing to plateaus overlooking the stunning fjords of the Norwegian coast, yet I couldn't suppress the anxiety and fear building inside of me. In preparation for this journey, I'd never honestly revealed to Sharon how dangerous this race could be. I have always made a commitment to her that my mountain indulgences would never put my life in danger, yet as race day drew closer I couldn't help but feel like I was violating something sacred between us. I had fallen victim to the "Kilian Effect" and I was now experiencing a psychological battle which subjected me to tremendous mood swings from excited bravado to fear and guilt; race day couldn't come and go soon enough.

On the day before the race, we had just arrived at race headquarters to collect my race kit when I noticed Kilian sitting at a desk working on logistics. Although I didn't want to appear starstruck, I sidled up to him and asked him to pose with me for a photo, and we then chatted for several minutes about running and skiing in Canada.

There was nothing pretentious or elitist about this guy—he just carried himself like a perfectly normal person, because that is what he—and every ultra-runner—is like and that is why, above all else, this sport is so special. Mountain runners do not have egos and they do not care about appearances or accolades—what they do care about is pushing themselves to be as good as they can be and respecting all others who finish, whether ahead of or behind them. The professional runner who cruises through a rugged mountain course in ten hours receives no greater adulation from fellow runners and spectators than the last competitor who crosses the finish line in twice that time. After a few minutes, I bade farewell to Kilian and he wished me luck and success in the race. Meeting and talking with him was inspiring; however, it also served as a reality check as to what I was about to get myself into. It is one thing to have a chat with the greatest mountain runner on the planet; it is something completely different to embark blindly into his mountain world at the most extreme level.

What had I done?

THE TROMSØ SKYRACE is split into two separate races, a twenty-three- kilometre route which summits Tromsdalstinden mountain; and my race, a fifty-five-kilometre loop which continues over Tromsdalstinden and then traverses and summits the Hamperokken ridge and mountain. As I waited among the crowd of runners on race morning, I was in awe of the level of human physique about to take on these challenges. A couple of hundred Scandinavian specimens all looked remarkably similar: all about twenty-three years old and constructed from nothing more than long lean limbs and movie-star looks.

Once the race started and we made our way up the first climb of the day, I envisioned that their inner organs were also much the same: generally limited to hearts, lungs, and blood vessels the size of Coke cans! The ease with which they skipped up the mountain trail was fascinating and humbling to me as I pushed as hard and as sensibly as I could to not get too far behind the field. As it turned out, by the time I summited Tromsdalstinden and looked back at the course behind me, I was pleased to see that I had managed to stay ahead of about half the runners. I was a bit shocked, however, that when I started my descent down the back side of Tromsdalstinden, a race official informed me that I was only thirty minutes ahead of the cut-off time. If I were to make it to the next checkpoint within the required time, I would need to push myself much harder.

Descending this slope was a wild ride indeed, as the route began with an extremely steep face of loose rocks followed by a 200-metre snowslide which could only be navigated by sliding on my butt. As I was accelerating down this slope, trying with all my strength to prevent my legs from buckling underneath me and sending me tumbling down, I heard someone from above yell "ROCK!" followed immediately by a series of loose boulders the size of badgers flying past me. I couldn't believe how real the danger of being struck by one of these projectiles was—because, once the descent down this snowslide began, I was locked in and it was impossible to dodge anything coming at me from above. Luckily, I reached the bottom without taking a strike to the head and made my way through the valley floor and up the next steep ascent towards the famed Hamperokken ridge.

As I struggled up the last one hundred metres to a plateau at the start of the ridge, my focus was on a helicopter in the valley far below me. I assumed it was either guiding tourists through the remote beauty of the

Norwegian mountains and fjords, or possibly rescuing some stranded trekker who was lost or injured. But my focus quickly shifted back to the race, as a fellow runner informed me that we only had ten minutes to reach the plateau—where, if we were too late, race officials would enforce a cut-off that would deny us the opportunity to cross the ridge and send us back down the mountain in defeat with a horribly disappointing DNF.

I somehow found another gear and scaled my way up the final few metres, making it to the checkpoint with only one minute to spare; I was the last competitor to successfully reach the cut-off in time.

As I crawled up and planted my legs on the first flat ground I had touched in the last three hours, six other runners were waiting ahead of me, all quietly gazing at the ridge ahead. As I lifted my head to join them in surveying the terrain, the site that greeted me almost made me throw up!

The Hamperokken ridge and summit that I had been studying on YouTube for months was now right in front of me and I could not believe how NASTY and STEEP and REAL the whole thing was. This was the most extreme topography that I had ever seen and I was shocked at how different it looked. If I were a child, I would have been convinced that what lay ahead was actually the spine of a gigantic Stegosaurus… connected to the long neck and tiny raised head of a Brontosaurus!

My respiration and heart rate were now off the charts as I envisioned my weary legs trying to navigate this section of the course; it looked VERY dangerous! However, within moments I was able to regain control of my metabolism and was now in awe of the sheer beauty all around me. A glance back towards Tromsdalstinden revealed postcard images of rugged mountains, lush green valleys, turquoise lakes, and fairy-tale fjords. Turning back towards Hamperokken, I was now almost weeping as I began to fully appreciate the grandeur of this part of the world; it was truly inspirational.

Then, the cruel reality of the situation overtook us again, as the few of us who were yet to set foot on the ridge started to hear reports of what had just happened no more than a hundred metres ahead of us. Hillary, one of the race leaders and an experienced professional American trail runner, had lost her footing on a loose rock and fallen off the ridge, tumbling over large sharp rocks before coming to a stop fifty metres below. We later learned that she had suffered life-threatening injuries, but all we knew at the time was that the helicopter I had caught sight of a few minutes earlier was, in fact, an emergency helicopter summoned to rescue this runner from the remote valley beneath us.

After a brief moment of introspection and silence, one runner exclaimed that there was no way in HELL he was going out on that ridge, and simply turned around and began the slow descent back to the previous checkpoint.

"Yeah," said a second guy, "I don't need to go out there. I'm going back as well."

A third runner voiced his apprehension and followed the other two, saying that he had been out on the ridge once before and he wasn't going back out there again. I looked around and noticed one of the last two runners who was still with me glance out across the ridge and then look back directly at me.

"You prepared to do this?" I said to him.

With obvious reservations and hesitation in his voice, he said, "Yes."

I swallowed, took a very deep breath and replied, "I didn't come all the way from Canada to just look at that damn thing, so let's go."

The final runner still on the plateau approached and gestured that he would join us. The three of us accepted that with a very slow and cautious navigation of the ridge and summit, it was unlikely we would successfully meet the next cut-off in time and that, once safely down from the Hamperokken summit, our race would be over. We all came to Tromsø with the goal of completing the race, but if a DNF was to be coupled with the honour of conquering Hamperokken, then we would all be at peace.

Soon there were to be only three figures remaining on the course: a Canadian, a German, and a Frenchman—and for me at least, the next two hours were about to become the most incredible and intense moments of my life.

AS WE BEGAN THE RIDGE TRAVERSE, the enormity of the task immediately became clear: we had to climb straight up a small rock face and then straight down with absolutely nothing to hold on to. The view down each side of the ridge was almost beyond belief; both sides were virtually vertical walls of rock, with us on top navigating no more than a couple of feet of precarious trail. And when I say "trail," I really mean NO trail. There was the odd pink flag sticking up between rocks that was intended to guide the way, but out here racers were pretty much freestyling the whole time, with only the ominous and distant Hamperokken summit as our beacon. Thoughts of Hillary tumbling off of the ridge haunted me.

This up-and-down-the-slope pattern repeated itself several times before we arrived at a large void in the trail. The crevasse we were now facing spanned about three feet across and dropped perhaps fifty metres. To continue on with the race, we had to somehow leap across this chasm and plant our feet on the other side and immediately grab whatever rock we could to avoid rebounding back into the opening. This was the first time in my life that I was truly fearful about my mortality. It is difficult to put into words the dread occasioned by a simple task that under normal circumstances should be relatively easy, but when coupled with the prospect of falling to one's death somehow becomes crippling.

It was overwhelming to realize that this psychological battle would be the first of many similar trials I would be forced to endure over the next couple of hours. After quietly staring across and down for several minutes, it was time to move forward, so the German runner took a running leap, followed by me, and finally our French running companion. Once safely across the gap, we all turned and looked back at the passage of our first obstacle—then, with varying expressions of profanity in various languages, we began the slow and cautious trek toward the summit.

Within a few minutes we were faced once again with terrain not intended for human navigation. The highest and most exposed part of the ridge was impossible to cross, so we were forced to find a lower route across the vertical wall beneath us; a narrow ledge no more than twenty centimetres wide was our only accessible path. The only way to continue was to orient ourselves on the ledge with our faces pressed sideways against the wall and our hands sliding across the rock as we slid one foot next to the other in a slow and terrifying mountain shuffle. Everyone knows that in a situation like this, the prudent advice is to NOT. LOOK. DOWN. Yet, with faces turned, our peripheral vision was constantly registering the void behind and below us and it made forward progress painstaking and slow. Our bodies had to remain perfectly upright, as the prospect of leaning back slightly from the wall and having gravity take over to tragic ends was a very real possibility. Every muscle in my body was tense, and my mind was focused on every single breath and every single movement. It was an exercise in complete cerebral control, because letting my thoughts wander to anything other than survival would have been disastrous. Once we successfully climbed off the ledge and onto safer ground, my entire body felt flushed with relief and my mind cleared to let me once again process the route ahead.

Hamperokken summit loomed nearer and larger and I was now able to see small figures at the top. They looked like ants. I could not believe that I was somehow going to have to try to get up there myself. Soon, one of those ant-like figures appeared larger and it became apparent that someone was literally skipping across the rocks towards us. The figure dipped down into a small depression, then vaulted out like some kind of human mountain goat wielding a video camera on an extension pole.

"Killlliaaaan!" I yelled as he settled next to us with his camera still rolling. Kilian Jornet is a highly-paid athlete sponsored by mega-outfitter Salomon—he is their meal-ticket—but if anyone were to think that, at his own race, he spends the day receiving updates while promoting some new product in his VIP luxury hotel room and being pampered by corporate executives, they would be dead wrong!

For most of his adventures, Kilian flies solo and documents everything himself, producing some of the most amazing films out there, which is what he was doing on the mountain with us on this day. No support crew, no technicians, not even a bottle of water! As we were struggling, trying simply NOT TO DIE, Kilian was sprinting along the ridge and up and down the summit capturing race footage—oh, and this just after he had scaled down from the ridge to assist in the evacuation of the fallen American runner. It was humbling!

Chatting with Kilian up on that ridge seemed as natural as leaning over the fence sharing stories with a neighbour. His presence was calming and a welcome relief from the tension we had been experiencing for the last hour. Soon, though, we had to bid him farewell and we all shook our heads at his athleticism and his character; the guy is simply in a league of his own.

WE WERE NOW ABOUT HALFWAY to the summit, and the ridge was not getting any easier. Slow methodical crawling was the preferred mode of ambulation, although at times we actually found a safe route that was runnable. For a few brief moments I was able to experience the joy of authentic sky running and got a much-needed boost of confidence.

And confidence was critical, as our sprint across the ridge quickly ended with yet another vertical wall of rock. We now had to find a new method of scaling this obstacle. Reaching the next section of the course above this wall would require legitimate rock-climbing skills, of which I had none. I managed to climb up to a small ledge by assimilating the traditional skill set of a climber, maintaining three-point contact with the wall while pulling up with my hand clamped around a secure rock.

The next ledge was about four feet above me, so my plan was to continue with my previous methods. I reached up with my left hand and latched onto a secure rock, then stretched up to the right, wrapping my fingers around a small outcrop and pulling up with my arms and pushing up with my legs. Suddenly, my right hand came free and I twisted back to my left as I my feet fell down to the ledge I had just conquered. Loose rock tumbled past. I couldn't quite process the magnitude of what had just happened. If my other hand had also come loose or if either of my feet hadn't landed on the ledge, the consequences would have been tragic.

I needed to maintain my composure and my focus and regain control of my shaking body, just as I had on the precipitous ledge earlier on the course. I realized that I absolutely had to manage every aspect of my physical and emotional wellbeing if I were to avert disaster. I dared not wait any longer before trying another ascent, otherwise I might find myself frozen in fear.

However, each time I tried to find purchase on a rock with my right hand, the rock would fall away. This happened several times before I decided that I must improvise a new method of scaling to the ledge above me. I remembered reading about serious climbers who scaled vertical walls by surveying the face for small fissures in which they could insert two fingers, and then twisting them so the knuckles served as a wedge, which would allow the climbers enough leverage to pull themselves up.

At the time I first read about it, I thought this "wedge method" was insanely unreliable, but now I was about to give it a try. I managed to pry loose a few small rocks, exposing a finger-sized crack in the wall. As if I knew what I was doing, I jammed two fingers in the crack and twisted them so they (and by extension me), were now painfully secured to the mountain. Aside from obvious concerns about my hand pulling away under the full weight of my body, I also considered what might happen if I were to successfully pull myself up, but my fingers remained solidly fused in the crack. Would my body recoil and cause me to swing back to where I started—or worse, would my fingers release on the short descent and make me fall even farther?

Clearly, I was spending too much time contemplating the consequences, so I managed to choreograph a desperate leap requiring every possible muscle and joint that I had. On a count of three, I pulled and jumped and twisted and...landed firmly on the ledge above.

Holy Fuck!

AT THIS POINT, my two European comrades and I leaned against the wall and stared straight up at the last fifty metres leading up to the Hamperokken summit. We were all overwhelmed with the experience of the last two hours and now needed to find one last gear to haul our weary bodies up to the highest point of the race. We hadn't talked much so far, but now had the opportunity to find out a bit about one another. Thilo was a German in his mid-twenties, who now lived in The Netherlands working as a computer scientist. Pierre, a doctor from the French Reunion Island, appeared about ten years older. Upon hearing that Pierre was a doctor, I remarked that it was comforting knowing that if either Thilo or I were to fall off the mountain we would have immediate medical care.

"Oh yes," replied Pierre, "but I should tell you that I am a gynecologist, so my assistance might be limited!"

That brief moment of humour was exactly what the doctor ordered, and laughter seemed to purge all the nervous toxins from my body.

Pierre, Thilo, and I regained our focus and without any further hesitation began our final ascent of the day—to that grand pinnacle that had first captivated me many months ago.

Even with only about 200 vertical metres to go, reaching the summit was still painfully difficult and tormenting. The final approach required hand-over-hand climbing up a fixed rope secured (I hoped!) to a vertical face of rock. Not since junior high gym class had I experienced such a task, and it illuminated, once again, how something so "easy" could become anything but!

After hauling my aching body halfway up the rope with my eyes focused only on the grip of my two hands, I allowed myself to glance up and then down for a brief moment. The image that crept into my mind was that of exhausted and frozen climbers slowly and methodically hauling themselves up the famed Hillary Step on their final push to the summit of Mount Everest.

Although Hamperokken was proving to be SERIOUSLY challenging, it was no Everest and at that moment, I actually started to feel like a bit of a "poser." I was beginning to feel somewhat ashamed for thinking that the hardships I was enduring were in any way comparable to those climbers hanging off a frozen coiled strip of nylon at 29,000 feet! People regularly die up there, whereas I was really nothing more than a tourist having a bit of a rough day!

Then I thought, once again, of our Hillary and the emotions she must have felt just two hours earlier, at the moment she was about to tumble off the trail to her possible death. I'll bet fear was one of them! Challenges, hardships, danger, and—above all else—fear are relative and cannot be gauged against anything or anyone else; when someone chooses to put themselves in a situation where their perception of fear and danger feel real, then they are damn-well real and must be respected.

On many times throughout this day, my fear was very real but soon all that fear was swallowed up by pride as my eyes focused on the summit. Strength now returned to my arms as thoughts of falling to my death were pushed aside by a proud and primal conviction to succeed and conquer. At the moment, this was my Everest and I was not going to limp onto that summit like a wounded animal—I had worked too hard for this moment to have it be remembered as weakness. So, with one last mighty pull from above and push from below, Hamperokken, in its brutal entirety, was finally under my feet.

HAMPEROKKEN SUMMIT barely had room for half a dozen people, so I was resigned to standing in one spot, taking in the beauty of the magnificent northern land and seascape. It was difficult to reconcile how something so spectacular could be so tormenting. Looking down the summit wall and back across the ridge, the grandeur that I had admired two hours earlier was now even more spectacular. The sun was still shining, but had descended slightly lower towards the horizon, casting shadows outward across each undulation from the ridge. The cool air from the altitude and late afternoon hour brought with it a gentle wind and walls of mist that slowly embraced the ridge, as if Mother Nature were wrapping the craggy spine in a soft blanket. I imagined her whispers of praise to the rugged granite: "you did well today, my dear. Goodnight!"

I NOW TURNED BACK to where my two climbing mates were standing and watched Pierre strike a triumphant pose, while capturing his achievement in a selfie. He appeared to be crying! Tears began to well in my eyes, too, as I looked past Pierre to the north. Standing there, at the highest elevation in the most majestic mountain range above the Arctic Circle, I imagined that I was looking beyond the North Pole to the back side of the planet. The moment was surreal.

My water bottle had been empty for a few hours now and the next source of hydration was a stream halfway down the mountain, so the three of us decided it was time to leave. Descending Hamperokken still presented its challenges; the slope was extremely steep and, just as at Tromsdalstinden earlier in the day, covered in snow.

This slide was even more punishing, as in the direct midday sun the surface changed frequently from smooth ice to sharp seracs to slush. Upon descent, I would accelerate down the ice chute, then scrape over the shards which cut into my buttocks, and finally plow into the soft slush; it was physically exhausting.

Once the snow ended, I was able to step sideways and fill my water bottle from the flow of melted snow coming from the very ice we had just descended. Kilian had advised us in advance that all water in this part of Norway was clean and safe, so I had no reservations about drinking it. At that point of the day, my mind still had room for one brief moment of humour as I imagined that the only possible contamination in the water could very well be frozen shards of skin from runners' asses!

The seemingly simple task of just filling a water bottle, however, became a new and unexpected challenge, as the constant flow of water polished the rocks, making their surfaces very slippery. Being only partway down the mountain, I found the slope still very steep and, along with the frictionless rocks, the task of reaching my bottle into the water became extremely challenging. The fear that I had conquered just thirty minutes earlier was once again gripping my body and mind as the danger of losing my purchase and tumbling down the waterfall to the base of Hamperokken was, once again, very real! Through sheer luck and focused determination, I safely pulled my body back from the water and joined Thilo and Pierre in one final descent to the bottom. Now all that remained in our race was a pathetically clumsy traverse over a two-kilometre field of boulders, before dropping down through a beautiful forest trail which would bring us to the next checkpoint, where our time in Tromsø would come to an end.

Thankfully, Pierre's fiancée arrived at the checkpoint and drove our three broken bodies back to Tromsø, where we exchanged hugs and high-fives before setting off on our separate ways. While walking away, Thilo remarked that this was his first DNF, but in spite of his failure, on this day he felt more pride in his efforts than ever before in his life. I stopped to look at him one last time and just smiled: I felt exactly the same way.

A SHORT WALK THROUGH THE TOWN towards the finish brought me to a small hill overlooking the harbour where I knew, just as she is in every race, Sharon would be waiting for me. With bruised and bloodied legs, I hobbled over to the knoll and embraced Sharon, while trying to hold back tears and guilt over how tormented she would have been if she had known the magnitude of the battle I had just endured. I will never do that to her again.

Eleven

I Think I'm Going to Kathmandu

Tromsø and the Hamperokken ridge and summit were really extensions of what I had previously thought had been my ultimate trail-running adventure, that being my time in the Himalayan Mountains with Ujesh several years earlier.

This story actually began towards the end of my teaching career, when I spent a considerable amount of time with my friend Blair, talking at length about our respective passion for trekking in Nepal, and our desire to one day hike to Mount Everest. We had both been avid readers of all things Everest for many years and Blair, being a few years older than I am, had set a personal goal of trekking to Everest Base Camp right after he retired from teaching. In preparing for his adventure, Blair would regularly invite me to his planning meetings with two other recently retired teachers, hoping to entice me to join the group. His trip was planned for April, so short of quitting my job, there was no way I could go, and just listening to him describe his trekking plans was excruciating.

At that point in my life, I had just started running trails in a forested, hilly area close to where I live. The Brandon Hills, as they are known, constitute a true yet hidden geographic gem. In the absolute middle of the Canadian prairies lies this small bump rising out of the surrounding wheat fields, which compresses within its borders well over fifty kilometres of spectacular single-track forest trails.

After a couple of years of marathon running exclusively on pavement and concrete, I found myself captivated by this entirely new form of running on dirt, grass, and rocks. To me it was a completely new sport, perhaps like switching from ping-pong to tennis. Running up and down these rolling hills was exhilarating, and it was during this time that I started to hear about mountain trail running and, to my disbelief, ultra-trail running, of distances up to one hundred miles.

I began reading books on trail running (*Born to Run* and others) and subscribed to trail running magazines. In one issue of a Canadian trail running magazine there was a short article about a woman from Quebec who had recently become the first Canadian to complete a trail marathon at Mount Everest. The reference was to the Tenzing-Hillary Everest Marathon, a race that was in its fifth year and was established to commemorate the first successful summit of Mount Everest by Sir Edmund Hillary and Sherpa Tenzing Norgay on May 29, 1953.

Each spring, a small group of runners from around the world trek up the mountain for fourteen days, arriving at Everest Base Camp on May 27. Here they spend two nights in tents under the Khumbu Icefall and then depart on May 29, running back via that same trekking route to arrive at the small village of Namche Bazaar anywhere from four hours later (for local elite Nepalese runners) to fourteen hours (for middle-aged portly adventure tourists with too much money).

I could hardly believe it, a Nepal trekking adventure AND a trail race at Mount Everest! I simply had to find out more, and I soon discovered that the following year, the organizers had established a companion race known as the Tenzing-Hillary Everest Extreme Ultra Marathon. This race was sixty kilometres in length and followed a different and more challenging route than the marathon. Just like Blair a couple of years earlier, I now began planning for my own Everest experience to mark my retirement.

My earliest retirement age of fifty-five was still a couple of years away, so I started making preparations to travel to Nepal in May of the year following my retirement. However, I soon realized that for financial and professional reasons, "Freedom 55" was not realistic; I knew I would likely need to teach for a few years beyond fifty-five and postpone my journey to Everest until I was fully retired. This realization was very deflating, but by a rather strange coincidence, a second passion of mine refocused my travel plans and brought me to Everest earlier than I'd first considered.

IN 1986, just two years into my career as a science teacher, the world was shaken by the news of the explosion at the nuclear power plant in Chernobyl, Ukraine. For the next thirty years, I read and studied as much as I could about this disaster, and regularly found a way to integrate Chernobyl into my teaching while seriously thinking about travelling to Ukraine to visit the Chernobyl site—it would be the ultimate professional development opportunity.

Immediately after the explosion, the wreckage was encased in a hastily built tomb that came to be known as "the sarcophagus." As the years passed, it became apparent to scientists around the world that Chernobyl was more than a one-time event, and if the radioactive rubble from the explosion was not permanently contained, further disasters would very likely occur. Consequently, a concerted effort was made to plan and prepare for construction of a second, larger, and more secure structure that would be built next to the original sarcophagus. When completed in 2014, this new structure would be slid over the top of the entire disaster site, sealing it for at least one hundred years.

The realization that my teaching career was coming to an end, and that my chance to travel to Chernobyl and visit the disaster site was also coming to an end, prompted me to act. I began contacting various departments at Chernobyl in an effort to acquire the credentials necessary to visit the site and make a more thorough inspection than that normally accessible to the new culture of "dark tourists."

I then submitted a detailed request to my superintendent and school board, asking permission for a leave of absence so I could travel to Chernobyl in May of 2014, arriving just before the scheduled installation of the new sarcophagus. I also proposed that, since I would already be travelling halfway around the world, then perhaps they would allow me to extend my leave so I could continue to Nepal and take part in the Everest ultramarathon.

My superintendent was very supportive of this proposal, so in October of 2013 I began making preparations for the adventure of a lifetime. To my shock and disappointment, I received a letter one month later from my Human Resources department, informing me that, despite the superintendent's recommendation, the school board had denied my request. In their opinion, an extended leave from my position as a chemistry and physics teacher, taken just one month before final exams, was unfair to the students and could put their graduating grades in jeopardy.

Undeterred, I promptly submitted a new request, asking if they would reconsider my leave for half that time. My rationale was that I could still travel to Chernobyl during my summer break, but my Everest running adventure could only happen on May 29. With a second push from my superintendent, the board approved my request, and within days I was registering for the race and booking flights to Nepal.

ON MAY 3, 2014, and after thirty hours of travel, I arrived in Kathmandu at 2:00 a.m. and was greeted by race organizers, who drove me through the city streets to the hotel where we would stay for two days before heading up into the Himalayan Mountains. The excitement of arriving in Nepal made sleep impossible, so I spent the next several hours wandering around the moonlit hotel grounds as the distant sounds of this new and exotic city filled the air.

Once daylight arrived I popped into the hotel restaurant, where I noticed a man sitting alone. With his shaggy blond hair and scruffy unshaven face, he had the look of a mountain runner, so I approached, asking if I could join him. Chris was in Nepal to run the marathon but was actually not a mountain runner at all, but rather a "Spartan"-type obstacle racer. He was from South Africa and, like me, had a keen interest in everything Everest. Unbelievably, this was to be his very first attempt at a marathon, kind of like a first-time road-biker entering the Tour de France! In spite of his lack of running experience, Chris just wanted to meet the challenge of the event.

I immediately liked Chris, as his excitement and positive character added to my own excitement about the days and weeks ahead. We sat for a couple of hours eating every possible Nepalese dish on the menu while sharing stories about our lives and the preparations we'd made for our travels.

One of my lasting impressions of Chris and my time in Nepal was his description of the childlike excitement he felt in the days leading up to his departure from home. A trip like this takes a significant amount of planning, and flights to Kathmandu are scattered at best. However, two days before his scheduled departure, he was somehow able to book a flight one day earlier than planned.

As he explained to me, he was unable to sleep or eat or think about anything else, and just had to get to Nepal as soon as possible. He said he felt like a child in the days leading up to Christmas. I had been feeling exactly the same way, so it was very satisfying that this kindred spirit was the first person I came to know on the trip.

Chris would be running a different race than me—he the marathon, and me the ultramarathon—and he would also be trekking up the mountain with a different group of runners and following a different route. I would, however, get the chance to see him again, as his group and my group would ultimately meet at the same place on the trail about ten days later.

AFTER WANDERING WITH CHRIS around Kathmandu for the afternoon, I returned to the hotel and introduced myself to Doug and Christine from Brazil, two of my new trekking partners. Just as with Chris earlier, we shared stories about ourselves over dinner, and talked about how excited we were to begin our trek up the mountain the following morning. I had met the final three members of our team earlier in the day—Ruth, a single Kiwi traveller, and Murray and Estelle, also from New Zealand—so our group was now set, and we prepared to spend the next three weeks together on Mount Everest.

When I registered for this event, I imagined that any race with the name "Everest" in its title would convey some serious "star power" and draw numerous elite runners from around the globe. Although additional runners would be joining us at Base Camp for the start of the race, I was surprised to learn that the six of us were the only entrants to have registered for the entire trekking experience and the race, and none of us, as far I could gather, were anything other than "ordinary." It appeared to be an exclusive club: a level playing field, where no one knew each other, and one that I was extremely proud to be a part of.

Settling into my room that night, I was consumed in both body and mind by the anticipation of our departure into the mountains the following morning. Our plan to ascend to Everest Base Camp would begin with a notoriously perilous flight from Kathmandu to an airport at the small village of Lukla, located halfway up the mountain.

The reason for Lukla's fame can be found via any Google search of the world's most dangerous airports. Lukla takes the number one spot on this list because its short runway, which begins just metres in front of a steep mountain face, must be navigated with an equally steep approach as small planes descend down through the valley.

Once the wheels touch down, normal braking would be insufficient to bring the craft to a stop on the short runway before the plane crashed into a large rock face at the runway's terminus. Consequently, the runway has been integrated into the natural steady incline of the topography, utilizing the forces of gravity to bring the plane to a stop. Pilots have one shot at getting this right, as there is no room for a second approach.

Landing at Lukla turned out to not be terrifying at all, but rather quite exhilarating, and as we touched down I began laughing with delight. I could hardly believe that I was now in the middle of the greatest mountain range in the world. I walked into a small lodge next to the runway and wandered through the tiny kitchen, where a few local women and girls were preparing food for trekkers. I carried the hot latte they made me out to a deck looking out over the village, and the mountains and valleys surrounding me; it was a scene more rugged, colourful, and exotic than anything I had previously imagined.

After savouring both the view and this delicious beverage, I made a phone call to Sharon and chatted for a few precious minutes, with my body literally shaking with excitement and anticipation of the weeks ahead. Once we left the region of the airport and our trek actually began, the first thing that made me realize I was now in a place far removed from anywhere I had ever been before was the complete absence of sounds from vehicles. With the exception of a few barking dogs, some clucking chickens, and yak bells, everywhere we walked we encountered complete silence.

I realized, of course, that there would be no roads or cars at this elevation, but our first exposure to this level of quietude was somehow still quite remarkable. The next fourteen days would be spent trekking in this stillness, up a seventy-kilometre route to our final destination at the base of Mount Everest, and the start of the Everest Extreme Ultra Marathon.

WHAT FOLLOWED BECAME A STORY within this story of the man I called Ujesh, a young, nameless, nomadic Himalayan angel who would guide me through some of the most incredible experiences of my life.

Twelve

A Guide and His Umbrella

My time with Ujesh began about halfway through the race, near the village of Pangboche. Here, an intersection in the trail guides marathon runners farther down the mountain, and ultramarathon runners back up the mountain. WAY up! I stopped for a drink of water on the trail and was immediately surrounded by a group of Japanese tourists. Dressed in unconventional trekking gear, and running down the mountain, I must have looked very peculiar to them. One after one, each trekker would approach and place their arm around me and pose with a "thumbs up" while the rest of the group snapped photos. It felt oddly pleasing to have the experience of being a "tourist attraction" in this foreign land.

Once the photoshoot ended, I began the long ascent up several kilometres to a pass just above our next aid station at the village of Phortse. Soon a young Nepalese man (perhaps still a teenager), carrying an umbrella and dressed simply in jeans, a windbreaker, and sneakers began running with me. Moments later, we were joined by two of his friends and we all scrambled up the trail together. I had no idea why these three locals were choosing to run with me; I gathered that they just wanted to join in and experience some of the "fun" of the event.

After about thirty minutes, the two friends gave me high fives and peeled off, leaving me and my mystery mate running together. He didn't speak much English, but there really wasn't any need to communicate, as the trails were now clear of the snow that had fallen earlier and I was focused on just pushing myself up the steep slope. I did gesture to him that he could leave me alone, but he insisted on staying with me.

Periodically, I would stop for a drink of coconut water and force down a bite of chocolate. Ujesh, the name that I will forever remember him by, carried no food or water with him, and when I offered him some he refused. An hour later I offered again, and this time he quietly and politely accepted. I couldn't understand why he was still with me when he was clearly becoming thirsty and hungry.

As the afternoon progressed and we arrived at Phortse, I was beginning to feel the effects of the previous few days on the mountain and the lack of food in my system. We stopped for a rest at the aid station, where I bought a couple of bottles of Coke from the Sherpa man (I believe his name was Rita) who owned the teahouse in which we had stayed a few days earlier.

At this point in the day, I was reminded of my previous visit with Rita a week earlier, and the realization I had had then about just how pedestrian my adventure really was by local standards. One night, while finishing dinner, Sherpa Rita and I had engaged in a conversation where I learned much more about his life. He explained to me that serving guests like me in his teahouse was, like for many other Sherpas, a means to earn a small income to supplement his work as an Everest guide.

Rather shyly, he explained to me that a few weeks earlier he had successfully guided clients to the top of Everest, his ninth successful summit. I asked him about that season's tragedies on the mountain: the death of a Canadian climber near the summit, and the loss of many other climbers and guides in an avalanche lower down on the mountain.

Shockingly, Rita told me that he had actually passed right over the dead Canadian on his summit push and had helped rescue the living and recover the dead in the avalanche zone on the way down. As my heart rose into my throat, he continued his story, telling me that every year he witnesses death on the mountain—and knows that one day his time may come—but his is the life of a Sherpa guide. All this while making repeated trips back to the kitchen to bring me fresh hot tea—as if somehow my presence were worthy of his service!

BACK IN THE PRESENT, it was time for me to leave and continue with the race, so I offered a Coke to my young companion, gave him 500 rupees, and shook his hand while trying to thank him with limited words and gestures. It had been very helpful having Ujesh with me for the previous three hours, but I was now preparing for the incredibly difficult ten-kilometre uphill trail that loomed above me, and I felt I needed to get into a rhythm and move ahead alone. I had only five hours to reach the next checkpoint at small area called Nha-La, and I was starting to worry that I might not make it in time. This would have been devastating for me, as I had to reach this checkpoint by that five-hour deadline in order to continue and finish the race in one day.

Rather than returning along the trail back to where we had started, I was startled when Ujesh grabbed his umbrella and pointed up the mountain. I tried to get him to go back but he insisted on staying with me. I was able to ask him how far he planned to go and he murmured, "Namche". I didn't quite understand, so I asked him again and this time I heard him clearly say in broken English, "NAMCHE. One runner, one guide to the finish in Namche." This guy was going to stay with me all the way to the end.

In a strange way, I was a bit disappointed knowing that I would not be alone for the rest of the race. Part of my excitement in preparing for this adventure was the anticipation of the time I would spend alone, experiencing the challenge and beauty of the Himalayas myself. I like being alone in nature, and this race would place me in a state of solitude matched by few places on earth. I wanted to experience everything at my own pace and on my own terms, and if I wanted to sing or swear, I wanted to be able to do so without annoying or offending anyone else.

Now I had to be on my best behaviour, and felt obligated to "socialize" with this stranger. I soon realized, though, that having a local Nepalese porter guide me through some of the most challenging terrain in the Himalayas would be considered by most as a good thing, so I sucked it up and continued with my race. Ujesh and I were now a team, and would remain so for the duration of the route.

During our first few hours together on the trail, I noticed that whenever I slowed down, Ujesh would momentarily pass in front of me to my left, and then quickly slip back behind me so I could not see him. He continued doing this for the rest of the race, and I surmised that Ujesh was always aware that this was my experience, and accordingly acted out of respect for that sensitivity. This may have seemed like a simple gesture on his part, but it filled me with respect for him and encouraged me to continue running and finish—for myself, but also partly for him.

This upcoming stretch of the route was the signature section of the race. Website promotion of the event boldly described this section as the "world's longest and highest-altitude uphill trail running section." When my mates and I had viewed this part of the trail from across the valley a few days earlier while trekking to Base Camp, we had all commented on not only how exposed it was, but also how it appeared to be a route that we could actually run and not just walk.

However, once I was actually on this route, it quickly became apparent how steep, dangerous, and totally un-runnable it was. The terrain in the race had been technical and challenging all along, but now the trails were also covered in periodic snowslides from the snow that had fallen over the last few days. These patches of snow, and the steep slopes, made finding a safe path extremely difficult.

The snow was about two feet deep and had become very icy and slippery during the course of the day. At one point I was able to follow directly behind a yak as it made its way up the mountain. Every yak step was followed by a human step, and if it had been necessary I could have grabbed his tail and hung on for the ride.

Pushing through these snowslides was physically and mentally exhausting. Looking down onto the rocky valley floor 1000 feet below made me extremely nervous as I cautiously placed one foot in front of the other, and it was at this point in the race that I first felt the umbrella.

As Ujesh walked behind me, he would regularly tap me on my downhill side, encouraging me to focus on shifting my weight up the slope. This simple gesture really made a difference in keeping me focused on my safety. On one occasion, I placed my foot on an unstable section of snow and ice and momentarily started to slide downhill. In an instant, Ujesh moved directly beside me so that he was downhill from me. Throughout the remaining slippery sections, he would continually place himself in a position where he could physically push on me with his hand and shoulder, thereby forcing my momentum up, rather than down.

You don't have to be a rocket scientist to realize that the force applied to me uphill resulted in the same force pushing him downhill. This guy was doing so much more than simply guiding or keeping me company—he was assuming responsibility for my safety while risking his own at the same time. My murmurs of thanks may have gone unnoticed, because he rarely responded with anything other than "OK, sir." My respect for Ujesh was growing at the same rate as the pain in my legs and lungs.

I had planned for this ten-kilometre section to take three hours to complete, which is about three times longer than any other ten-kilometre race I'd ever done before. I now found myself three hours in with only five kilometres behind me. With snow falling, temperatures dropping, wind blowing, and dark approaching, this was now becoming harder and more exhausting than I could have imagined.

I felt like anything but a fit trail runner at this point. I knew there was an aid station at the Thore tea house, perched on a remote mountain ledge about two kilometres ahead, so I held out some hope that in a short time I would be able to get some much-needed rest and fuel.

However, with every brutal ascent and every corner, my hopes of seeing this lodge faded; all that were ahead of me were more hills and even worse weather. I know that in long races every part of the trail seems longer than it actually is, but this was getting ridiculous. Pretty much everything a trail runner does not want to have happen in a race was now happening to me.

The weather and trails were dreadful and I was cold, dehydrated, malnourished, and exhausted. Added to that, partial blindness from the sun reflecting off the snow that had fallen earlier in the race—and on the previous two days at Base Camp—was now making it difficult to focus on the trail and was also giving me a terrible headache. Worst of all, and the thing that every runner fears the most, was the feeling of defeat and an almost overpowering urge to quit. I was not in a happy place.

Thirteen

Soup of the Day

Finally, Thore lodge appeared around the next corner, and there to greet us were the smiling proprietors. I bought a Coke and then asked if I could go inside and sit down. Once inside, I fell down onto a bench, propped my head in my hands and started to weep and shake. I felt like I was in a state of shock that wasn't ending; I couldn't lift my head up and I couldn't stop shaking. I was an absolute mess.

I'm sure my fragile state concerned the sweet Sherpa Lady, because she gently tried to get me to lie down in a room and cover up with a blanket. I politely refused, as I literally could not move. She left me alone initially—only to return three or four times in the next ten minutes to offer me hot tea. Again I refused, as I knew trying to put any food or liquid into my system was pointless: it would immediately just come back up and seriously mess up her tidy lodge floor.

I managed to glance around and noticed Ujesh sitting in the kitchen with Sherpa Lady and her husband. He never approached me, but he nonetheless sat in a position that allowed him to keep a watchful eye on me. I glanced toward the window and saw the snow and wind getting worse, which launched me back into my previous state of shaking and weeping, as I could not possibly imagine continuing with the race. I was still one or two hours away from the Nha-La checkpoint, and there was just no way that I could regain the strength and focus needed to carry on.

Not only was I not going to finish the race in one day, but I feared that I was not going to finish at all. I did not know what to do. I could turn around and find the shortest route back to Namche, or I could try to ask my guide to continue to Nha-La and inform the doctor stationed there that I was stuck in Thore and unable to continue.

Leaving the lodge and continuing the race at this point seemed impossible, so I considered the very real possibility that I might need to be assisted back to Phortse, where I could be evacuated by helicopter. This thought destroyed me. I thought of my friends, family, and students back home: their excitement for me and their confidence in my ability to finish this race. Having to give up now brought me to tears once again, as I thought of their disappointment in me. I was miserable and disgusted in myself for having fallen to this deplorable state. I had never felt worse in my life.

After another fifteen minutes or so of indulging in my own pathetic little pity party, I managed to pull the dry clothes from my Camelbak and find some comfort in feeling slightly warmer. Sherpa Lady once again approached with the offer of tea. I accepted this time, and sat back down to sip it as she went back to her kitchen.

Glancing in her direction, I noticed that Ujesh was still sitting and watching me while he ate a bowl of soup. I was happy to see he was eating something, as he must have been very cold and hungry and I couldn't stand the thought of dragging him out through the dreadful conditions anymore. His eyes continually fixated on me with every spoonful. A bit strange, I thought, but it was also very comforting to know that he and the Sherpa Lady were watching over me during my terrible time.

Drinking the cup of hot tea, I actually started to feel somewhat better. Sherpa Lady refilled my cup two more times and then, about forty-five minutes after arriving, I had the strength to stand up and walk. I followed her into her kitchen and sat beside Ujesh, while nursing my fourth cup of tea.

Sherpa Lady offered to make me some soup, which I initially declined, but then accepted a few minutes later. She jumped up and gathered a pot and water and various flavours of dry soup packets for me to choose from. I picked tomato, and then sat back to wait for my meal, absorbing the surreal scene in which I found myself.

The kitchen had a dirt floor, with walls of stone and mud, and there was a yak-dung fire burning in a stove in the corner. The snow was still blowing outside, and it was dark and dirty inside. The three Nepalese spoke with each other softly in their native language while I sat quietly, taking in everything around me. I had now recovered somewhat from my earlier pathetic state and was actually beginning to appreciate my current situation.

Here I was, in one of the most isolated places on the planet, surrounded by total strangers who were caring for me as if I were family. I had finally reached a destination that I had been dreaming about for most of my adult life and was in the middle of an extreme adventure that few people in the world will ever experience. And now I was devouring a simple bowl of tomato soup, which I may remember as one of the best dining experiences of my life.

Ujesh and I finished our soup, and then we sat, taking in the warmth and pungent smoke from the fire. I looked at him and asked him about the route to Nha-La. His gesture of two fingers confirmed with me that the doctor was about two hours away. He could see that I was considering moving forward, so the two of us now stood together and made the decision to continue. I didn't know what the next few hours would bring, but I had now found the strength and commitment to at least try and find out.

I thanked Sherpa Lady for her care and offered some money. She refused, but when I insisted, she finally accepted. It was 1000 rupees, about twelve U.S. dollars, and she reacted as if she had just won the lottery. She tried to give it back, but I refused. Finally, she gave me a big hug and insisted that her husband grab me some chocolate bars to take with me. I accepted one, we exchanged our final goodbyes, and with that, Ujesh and I returned to the mountain trail.

CLEARLY, IT IS A STRETCH to profess that these mysterious and beautiful Nepalese people saved my life, but I can say that they all contributed in a very real way to making me feel more alive than ever before. An hour after first collapsing at the lodge, I felt as though I had been awakened from the dead—and I just knew that once we left Thore, Ujesh and I would continue as one until the finish.

Thirteen

Kerosene Eggs

I should have known better than to allow myself to reach the state of despair in which I had found myself at Thore. My group and I had all been through this region while trekking eight days earlier, and we all acknowledged at the time how brutally difficult these trails would be during the race. I know that in every difficult race, success comes just as much from eating and drinking as it does from efficient running. Yet, in these extreme mountain conditions, I somehow allowed myself to reach a point of malnutrition, dehydration, and total exhaustion, from which I could not escape.

I was angry with myself that I could be so irresponsible. I had adequate chocolate, protein, water, and electrolytes with me, but I was just not disciplined enough to force myself to eat and drink regularly. Now, in my defense, and in defense of every other struggling runner on that day, the three days leading up to the race were unlike any other tapering period that a runner could ever experience, and this definitely had had a negative effect on race day. Gentle runs, lots of sleep, and carbo-loading were certainly not part of any of our pre-race routines.

REWIND TO THE MORNING OF DAY TEN of the pre-race trek, and a few days before the start of the actual race. As we prepared to leave the small village of Lobuche, a light and somewhat unexpected snowfall arrived in the region. I made a short video on my GoPro and commented that, being the one runner from a winter nation, I was prepared for the snow and cold. I boldly proclaimed that I was confident I could do well despite the conditions.

By the time we arrived at Gorak Shep four hours later, the skiff of snow that had started in Lobuche had accumulated to a foot of powder and was now seriously taxing our weary trekking legs and oxygen-starved lungs. Fog and mist began to sweep down through the Khumbu valley and envelop our little Sherpa village, creating a scene that could be mistaken for a spring storm in Banff.

My trekking mates, Ruth and Phil, joined me to hike farther up the Base Camp route, with the hope of finding a memorial for Rob Hall, a climbing expedition leader from New Zealand who had died in the infamous 1996 Everest disaster.

Our navigation skills, being as weak as our legs and appetites, made this pursuit unsuccessful, but we did stumble across something of even more significance to me. For the last year, I had kept a picture on my computer desktop of a tattered yellow and red sign sticking up out of the mountainside that read: "Way to Mount Everest Base Camp." Every day when I worked on my computer this picture would greet me, and seeing it always inspired and motivated me for this incredible journey.

As we were navigating our way through the snow and mist, my eyes caught a distant hint of yellow on a ridge about two hundred feet above us. As I climbed closer, I realized that this was the same sign I had been staring at for the last year. In clear weather, I suppose this sign could have actually provided some guidance to Base Camp trekkers, but in this blinding snow it seemed as remote and directionless as a sign guiding me to Mars. As little help as it was, I now remember this sign as one of the highlights of my Himalayan adventure. Back home, my computer monitor now greets me with a picture of myself standing beside that very sign—with a smile as big as Everest itself.

The continued snowfall and increasing impassability of the trail prompted us to head back to the village, a round trip of about three hours. Now, back at the lodge, sitting around the yak-dung stove, we were all wet, cold, and tired, but what's more, we were increasingly anxious for the next morning, the final push to Base Camp, where we would spend two days before the start of the race.

When I was preparing for this adventure, I had read that appetites get severely depressed at this altitude, and I had been noticing this for the last three or four days. What had started as a voracious appetite in Lukla ten days earlier was now reduced to a constant struggle to force down whatever menu item seemed least offensive.

Earlier in the trip, my meal selection had usually been dhal bat, a Nepalese lentil and rice dish, and lots of it. The thought now of swallowing even one grain of white rice brought about gag reflexes reminiscent of teenage drinking binges. My new default food choice now was egg omelettes. Generally, these were reasonably decent-tasting and cooked quite well. However, on this last night at Gorak Shep, a pronounced vile odour and taste of kerosene permeated the eggs, and Murray, my Kiwi friend, and I laughed and gagged as we struggled to finish our distasteful dinner. The question now was: which flavour of vomit was I most likely to tolerate and recover from—fossil-fuel eggs or white rice that brought to mind images of maggots?

IN ADDITION TO NOTORIETY for my ongoing culinary critiques, I was now also becoming known as the whiny Canadian who was too sophisticated for Nepalese toilets. But I used the foul facilities just as everyone else did: I simply commented daily on how disgusting they were.

When using these toilets, I could never quite figure out the proper squatting technique, nor could I reconcile myself to the practice of disposing of used toilet paper in a wastebasket and having it fester there for days on end. Every visit would bring tears to my eyes, and nausea to my stomach. (A note that my wife and friends would be quick to tell you that I am not one to openly discuss human waste management. I am still trying to find the strength to perform the off-putting task of obtaining a stool sample for colon cancer screening.)

Now, however, as we prepared to embark on the adventure of our lifetimes, toilet talk seemed to be at the forefront of many of our conversations, and my new friend Douglas from Brazil quickly became the Jerry Seinfeld of this new genre of comedy. His story about the onset of a bout of diarrhea during a marathon on a secluded beach in Brazil, and the creative use of his white Nike running cap, had me in stitches.

My utter disgust with Himalayan toilets descended to a new low when an overflowing and frozen toilet in our teahouse prompted Douglas' decision to bypass the toilet altogether and squat over the wastepaper basket to make a full deposit. If he hadn't been such a great guy, after this incident I would have never come within a metre of Douglas for the rest of the trip!

Toilet terror continued when, upon reaching Gorak Shep, I discovered that my headlamp was still under my pillow…in Lobuche! (I'd put it there to keep the batteries warm.) This was a problem for a couple of reasons, the most important being that a headlamp becomes critical when "race day" becomes "race night." However, of more immediate significance was the need for a lamp when visiting the latrine at night.

Lodges at this elevation become extremely cold at night and with no electricity for lighting, 3:00 a.m. toilet trips require full clothing and a headlamp. On this night, my bladder seemed distended to new limits, and with no headlamp I was forced to use my iPhone flashlight to guide the way to the facilities—which was functional to a degree, except that a phone is not designed to be strapped to one's head, thereby prohibiting freedom of the hands to perform other very necessary functions.

I should have just learned to stay in bed and pee into bottles like Doug and Christine, dumping the waste in the morning, but I somehow found this technique more offensive and more trouble. So there I was, in a cold and dark Himalayan bathroom, with my three layers of pants down around my ankles, one hand holding my phone light, and the other guiding a gallon of urine into a hole in the floor—a hole surrounded by urine and feces left by previous trekkers who had also suffered from frozen hands and blurred night vision.

Apparently, the laws of gravity still apply at that altitude, and in one fatal instant, my phone fell into the toilet hole with a constant flow of urine flooding down on top of it. With my bladder still emptying, I reflexively dropped to my knees (soaking up urine slush) and plunged my arm down into the abyss to grab my phone.

There are certainly other things I could have imagined that were more tragic than this, but at that moment, pulling my phone out of a dreadful feces-encrusted hole from hell in the midst of frozen darkness was about as bad as it could get. I returned to my room, and with the aid of a couple of packets of baby wipes to disinfect the phone, I discovered it was still working. I could have summited Everest and still not felt as elated as I did that night, knowing I had rescued my phone from that putrid pit.

When the kerosene eggs from earlier in this day forced me to make a return trip for my one and only brief bout of diarrhea (quite fortunate actually, considering I later found out my friend Chris, trekking in a different group, had fifteen in ONE day!), I left my phone in my room and accepted that this cold and dark disaster had the potential to be equally unpleasant.

My memory of the next ten minutes or so is a bit foggy (I may have blocked it out), but I do know that this night of terror ended with many more baby wipes and soiled clothing covering the floor. For perhaps twisted reasons, I carried myself with pride for the rest of the trip, knowing that I now had the best toilet stories. My mates were impressed.

Fourteen

The Bowels of Base Camp

Although our schedule was tight, the following morning I was joined by Douglas, Christine, Ruth, Phil, and our Sherpa, Mindu, for a climb up Kala Patthar to an altitude of over 18,000 feet: the highest point of our trip. It is at the summit of Kala Patthar that the classic view of Everest reveals itself.

Struggling through even more overnight snow, we reached about halfway up the mountain before Douglas and Christine decided to head back down. Two days earlier, they had aborted their climb above the village of Dingboche and now, once again, they couldn't find the strength or motivation to continue. I was getting a bit concerned about them.

But Ruth, Phil, Mindu, and I continued our push to the summit, spending an hour in conditions that obscured our hopes of an Everest view, but that nonetheless provided an incredible experience. Kala

Patthar is one of those places I had read and thought about for years, and finally reaching this iconic location was a life-changing experience. We returned to Gorak Shep about three hours later, cold and tired, and began packing our gear for the final trek to Everest Base Camp.

We set out for Everest Base Camp the next day after lunch, and followed a difficult path that, as we trekked it, was being covered in even more snow. About halfway to Base Camp we traversed a ridge that normally would be rocky, challenging, and beautiful. On this day, however, the ridge was covered in two feet of snow and the visibility was very poor, which made the path no longer merely challenging, but extremely dangerous. Tight and narrow icy trails gave way to steep slopes falling 200 feet down to a dozen or so snow-covered yaks in the valley floor below. I was convinced that someone was going to tumble down and join that herd before the day was done.

There was no joking among runners on this trek, as the seriousness of the situation kept everyone alert, focused, and a bit fearful. Thankfully, my worries did not materialize and everyone made it to Base Camp safely, where the scene that greeted us upon our arrival simply made me laugh out loud.

Scattered around this desolate place were fifty yellow tents perched on a ridge under the notorious Khumbu Icefall. The tents were covered in snow, and people were walking through the knee-deep drifts, falling regularly as they tried to navigate paths to them that just didn't exist. Snow continued to fall and, coupled with the wind and the mist, made the place look like some kind of Siberian Gulag labour camp.

I spotted a few small blue tents also scattered throughout the camp and realized these would be our toilets for the next two days and nights. I now imagined there would be an entirely new set of toilet stories in the days ahead.

Our lead Sherpa, Pasang, informed us that we shouldn't sleep in our tents alone. First, it was so cold and wet that two people were needed to generate adequate body heat throughout the night. Also, as the snow continued to fall overnight, he advised us that tent companions should take turns knocking the snow off their tents to prevent them from collapsing and to allow for adequate ventilation.

Ruth and I were the only single travellers in our group, so that night I got to share a tent with my young Kiwi companion. I commented that it was unlikely that many other fifty-four-year-old married men have had the opportunity to sleep with a twenty-five-year-old woman at Everest Base Camp! Ruth laughed when I suggested that sleeping with me was probably not high on her list of things to do while in Nepal, either!

After a miserable dinner in a cold, wet mess tent, Ruth and I crawled into our home away from home and prepared ourselves for the night ahead. At this point it was only 6:00 p.m., and still twelve hours away from breakfast and daylight.

SOMEHOW RUTH seemingly has the capacity to hold urine for days at a time, while only a couple of hours into our night, I couldn't suppress the need for a full toilet experience. The thought of struggling fifty metres through the snow to the toilet tent disturbed me greatly. My mind was clearly not right, as by the time I had struggled halfway to the toilet, I realized that I had not brought the headlamp my Sherpa had loaned me earlier.

It was dusk, so I could still manage to find my way along some of the paths through the snow, but not without falling several times along the way. The toilet tent was about what I expected: three feet square, with flat rocks piled around a small opening that dropped down to a barrel below, and a thin curtain for a door that flapped open in the wind. At least the dark and cold air suppressed the repugnant sight and smell. I couldn't help but feel bad for the unfortunate porter who had to carry this barrel back down the mountain trail two days from now.

My Nepal toilet struggles continued, as I could not figure out a way to squat over this sewage hole without doing serious damage to the only dry and warm clothes I had with me. I made the decision to remove my boots and four layers of underwear and pants and do my business half-naked—hoping like hell that I didn't slip and knock a boot into the cesspool below.

What should have taken no more than a few minutes at worst now became a thirty-minute struggle to complete the wretched task and get dressed, while trying to keep my frozen ass from poking out into the cold Everest wind. I exited the toilet to discover that darkness had fallen, and I had no idea where my tent was located. All I knew was that it was perched right next to a cliff under the icefall; which, of course, was totally obscured by the snow and dark.

The prospect of a missed step and a tumble down a crevasse at the base of Mount Everest while clutching toilet paper in my hands was not one I wanted to see realized. I considered yelling for Ruth, but my pride made me suppress that urge, so I just began moving in a direction that I hoped would lead towards my tent, but safely away from the dangers of the icefall.

The walk back was comical: slipping on a rock was followed by falling onto a tent, and then falling face-first into the snow. Every tent was covered in snow, and the mountain storm and darkness forced me to climb up to a ridge so I could hopefully regain my bearings. After descending from the ridge, I collided with several more tents before finally locating my own, where I collapsed inside, in a scene reminiscent of the popular Everest disaster book *Into Thin Air.*

Although I was frozen and exhausted, I was, at least, able to find some pleasure in knowing that my description of the past hour's travails of mountain madness provided Ruth with a brief moment of laughter in an otherwise dreadful night.

***

AND DREADFUL WAS AN APT DESCRIPTION—if not a considerable understatement—for the night ahead. The cold and dampness brought on constant shivering, while the altitude and limited ventilation made me bolt upright on several occasions in a state of anxiety, gasping for every available molecule of oxygen. Aside from the truly awful conditions inside the tent, what was happening outside made the experience even more miserable.

With our backs turned to each other and each of us silently curled up, hugging every fibre of clothing and sleeping bag we could grab, Ruth and I tried to focus our bodies and minds on warmth and sleep. The thick blanket of snow covering us, and everything else in this expansive, high-altitude setting, muted virtually every sound. Suddenly, a thunderous roar broke through the silence and made us both sit up and turn to each other, with the same thought in mind: HOLY SHIT! AVALANCHE!

The sound of snow and ice cascading down a nearby mountain was alarming—and for good reason. Just one month earlier, a major avalanche had struck the Everest region just a few hundred metres above our tents, killing sixteen Sherpas and porters. And just one year after my journey there another major avalanche, triggered by a massive earthquake, made a large wall of snow funnel down the Khumbu valley, where it crashed over Base Camp, burying tents and climbers in our exact location.

My understanding was that Everest Base Camp is generally a pretty sublime place…unless you happened to be stuck in a tent, in a snowstorm for the ages, during a time when two of the deadliest avalanche events in the region's history had occurred. There were to be no sweet dreams on this night!

We had been hearing distant avalanches along our trekking route for the last few days and, for the most part, had simply marvelled at them; there was no fear. The feeling now, while stuck inside our frozen tent in complete darkness, was quite different. The ominous sounds continued for the rest of the night—which made sleep even more difficult—but at least the avalanches were continuous, allowing us to gradually become desensitized to their danger.

Eventually, I was able to generate enough body heat inside my sleeping bag to allow me to slip into a very light sleep. This was temporary, however, as once again, I was jolted out of my sleeping bag by not only the sound of another avalanche, but by the violent shaking of our own tent as well.

The storm was continuing throughout the night, and our tent had accumulated a thick layer of ice and snow. The situation had become dire enough that our Sherpa leaders had directed the guides and porters to walk around our camp for the entire night knocking snow and ice from the tents. Their preferred method was to grab the ropes that secured the tent to the ground and to shake them violently, thus flapping the tent canvas enough to send the snow flying off.

If the situation had not been not so serious, I could have imagined these acclimatized mountain men gathered around a warm stove in their own barracks, devising a sinister plan. Like a gang of devious schoolboys, they would silently skulk around from tent to tent—shaking them violently and scaring the crap out of the frozen runners inside—then run off into the night, slapping each other's backs and laughing with delight.

AFTER SPENDING ABOUT TWELVE cold and sleepless hours in our icy sarcophagus, morning finally arrived—where I discovered three more feet of snow blocking our exit. I struggled to put on my frozen boots, kicked my legs through the wall of snow, then crawled out, drawing in my first breath of fresh air since that terrible toilet trip the night before.

The snow was still falling, and I couldn't believe how our camp had changed. What had looked like a rather "normal" mountain winter landscape the day before had now become something out of a "Wild Weather" segment from the Discovery channel. As a Canadian, I was a bit shocked with the weather we were experiencing; I couldn't begin to imagine what Ruth and the rest of my Kiwi and Brazilian friends were thinking.

One by one, battered runners began emerging from their own tents and clumsily wandering off to the mess tent for breakfast.

"Mess" was the operative word that morning, as everyone felt beat up from the previous day and night. Murray lightened the oppressive mood somewhat with the tale of his own toilet trip early in the morning, and the image of Murray tripping over tents and rocks and falling face-first into the snow (just as I had) has me laughing to this day.

I was, of course, concerned about his wellbeing, but as he continued to talk about his feeling of impending death as, freezing cold and exhausted, he pushed through four feet of snow gasping for oxygen, it made me think of my own experience and I couldn't help but find levity in his trauma. The image of Murray finally inside his tent with Estelle, his wife and nurse, desperately trying to get him to breathe and control his shaking, just added to the twisted state of hypoxic humour we all seemed to enjoy.

Fifteen

Blinded by the Light

While we were finishing breakfast, Pasang, who one month earlier had been in this exact location during the deadly avalanche directly above us, advised us that the dangers of all the new snow meant that it was necessary to evacuate and return to Gorak Shep immediately.

Passang explained that there would be many dangers in staying and starting the race at Base Camp. The continued snowfall could actually block access to the race trails below Base Camp, runners faced the serious risk of hypothermia, the deep snow made moving around camp very dangerous, and the race trail would be in an avalanche zone once the sun came out and the mountain walls warmed up. It was disappointing accepting that we would not be starting the race at Base Camp, but it was clear that we needed to leave.

Because we all needed to evacuate together, many of the runners took on the responsibility of carrying gear that would normally be carried by our porters. The porters were required to haul down all the tents, toilets, and cooking equipment, so their loads had to be limited. Many of us quickly began assisting the porters in digging out and packing the tents. This was physically exhausting, and when it was time to leave, most of us were ready to crawl back in the tents we had just packed and go to sleep.

The walk back through the snow to Gorak Shep had many people quite concerned. As exhausted runners stopped to rest, others behind them were urging, if not demanding, that they continue, as we were in an avalanche zone and needed to evacuate the area quickly This debate among the retreating runners continued for several hours, until we finally reached the flat trail leading back to Gorak Shep. Now, when I think back to the earthquake and avalanche tragedies around the time of my travels in Nepal, I am left to wonder if the conditions we had found ourselves in could have just as easily resulted in us becoming the next tragic victims of this unforgiving landscape.

ABOUT TWO HOURS LATER, with all of our heads down on lodge tables from exhaustion, a Dutch marathoner came running in, asking if anyone knew Douglas and Christine. She told us that they were still out on the trail with no water or food, suffering from snow blindness and complete exhaustion.

First, Ruth sprinted out on the trail; I followed, carrying Coke, water, and chocolate. Murray and Estelle joined us, proclaiming that we were a team, and that we would all be together through good and bad.

We found Doug and Christine moving very slowly on the trail. They were being assisted by Phil, but they were looking terribly sick and in need of more assistance. Neither of them could see very well; in the confusion of departing Base Camp they weren't able to locate their sunglasses, and they were now suffering from snow blindness. Christine especially appeared to be in very bad shape, and we all gathered around her and guided her back to the lodge.

Upon reaching the lodge, both Christine and Doug began to recover somewhat with the administration of hot tea and warm clothes. Douglas teared up as he thanked us for helping him and his wife and expressed how proud and honoured he was to be among all of us. This was a moment in the trip that I will never forget.

Later that night, we were happy to see that Douglas and Christine were feeling much better; our group had become quite close over the previous two weeks, and we genuinely cared about each other.

***

IT WAS NOW the night before the race and marathoners and ultra-marathoners gathered together in the lodge for a final feast of pasta and soup. The pasta was plain white bland spaghetti, but considering my memories of eggs and dhal bat, it was perhaps my best meal in the preceding week.

All the runners were now very excited, as race day was finally upon us. It had been an amazing trekking experience up to now, but we were all are here for the race and the anticipation around the room was palpable. Everyone was cold and wet and tired from the previous two days, but all of that was suppressed as the pre-race rituals of packing and repacking race gear dominated our thoughts and actions.

The ultra-marathon was set to begin at 6:00 a.m., so we planned to get up around 4:00 a.m. to finish packing and eat our pre-race breakfast. After I woke up at 4:00 a.m., I wandered the halls and banged on the doors of the rest of the runners. It was still very dark, but as I got to Doug and Christine's room I noticed Douglas standing outside looking somewhat disoriented.

"Mark," he said, "we need the doctor. Christine and I cannot see again and we have bad headaches and are feeling very sick. Christine is in the room throwing up and can't get out of bed." I left Douglas in the hall and went to check on Christine. She was sitting on the bed with glazed and watery eyes. She appeared to be very cold and sick. I sat beside her to offer some comfort and then noticed my feet sliding on the floor beside the bed.

"Mark," she said to me in a frail voice, "I am sorry. I have been throwing up macaroni and garlic on the floor. I could not get up to go to the toilet." My slippers were now coated in pasta puke, and I realized I would now need to pack these slippers into my bag in their soiled state, because time was now moving quickly towards 6:00 a.m. and it would be a struggle to get myself ready for the race, let alone take the time to wash my footwear.

I was not concerned as, at this point in our journey, cleanliness had become a lower and lower priority. I managed to locate some eye drops the doctor had given me earlier in the trip and brought them to Christine. Being a doctor herself, she was reluctant to use them without knowing what the medication was, so I ran out to the dining room where other runners were now having breakfast. I could not see the small writing on the bottle, so I asked Ruth to spell the name of the medication. With this knowledge, I ran back to Christine and gave her the drops, while trying to remember the spelling of the medication. Time was now slipping by as quickly as my feet on Christine's vomit.

Christine crawled back into bed, and I went back out to the hall to find Douglas. Our doctor had left the day earlier to set up the medical checkpoint along the trail at Nha-La. We were told that a different marathon doctor was still with us in the lodge, but we had no idea where his room was located.

I found one of the marathon porters and asked him to help us locate the doctor. If the situation hadn't been so serious for my Brazilian friends, it would have been quite comical; the Sherpa and I leading a blind man through the cold, dark halls, knocking on doors and asking if a doctor was in the house.

At one point, someone in an incoherent state of morning fog told Douglas the doctor was at the summit of Kala Patthar. This just added to Douglas's own already depleted and disoriented condition, as we now tried to make sense of why the doctor would be 1000 feet above us on an isolated summit. All we were able to discern was that the doctor wasn't in the lodge and wouldn't be back for a few hours.

I felt terrible for Christine and Douglas, as they were both very sick; so sick that they ultimately made the difficult decision to not participate in the race. They had been such great travelling companions, and their motivation and passion for running had been very uplifting for all of us. In a short time, they had become close friends, and I wish I could have done more for them during this very difficult time.

Earlier in the trip, Douglas had mentioned that he had brought along an extra Brazilian T-shirt that he wanted to give to someone who had become friends with them and who had made an effort to help them during their adventure. I was quite humbled when he offered this gift to me. They are both very patriotic, and this was a very significant gesture on their part. I regret that in the turmoil of that morning, I didn't dig that shirt out of my bag and wear it during the race, in their honour.

Douglas and Christine had been very committed in their preparations for this race and had been documenting all of their experiences in the hopes of writing a book about this and some of their other running adventures. Sadly, it now appeared that the final chapter would be something other than a triumphant finish.

Later that morning, the doctor finally arrived and provided some assistance to Doug and Christine. Eventually, they were evacuated from Gorak Shep by helicopter, and then transported back to the finish in Namche. It was quite comical getting together with Doug and Christine after the race to watch the video of the two of them being led by Sherpas on each side towards the helicopter. Douglas laughed at this image, as they looked very much like hostages being kidnapped and hauled away to some secret location.

FINALLY, 6:00 A.M. ARRIVED and we all lined up at the start line. The sun was still behind the mountains, and it was freezing cold. I was dressed in several layers of pants, shirts, and jackets, along with sunglasses, a hat and scarf, trekking poles and gloves, a hydration vest packed with extra warm clothing and food, a belt with more food and coconut water, and my GoPro camera mounted on my chest. I looked like I was about to land on the moon! As I glanced down the start line at the Sherpa competitors, I saw they were simply wearing shorts and shirts. Clearly, they were not planning on being out as long as I was!

AND SO, AFTER TWO YEARS of planning and twelve days of trekking, my dream of running the Everest Extreme Ultra Marathon finally began. Within one hundred metres of the start, the reality of the extreme conditions we were facing quickly became apparent. A small uphill section forced me to slow down to a crawl, as I desperately tried to keep my heart and lungs from exploding. The air was thin, cold, and dry, the ground was covered in snow and ice, and I pushed forward: not knowing that this was just the beginning of fifteen hours of torture and—ultimately—triumph.

The Everest Extreme Ultra Marathon headquarters, and my hotel while staying in Kathmandu, Nepal.

The world's most dangerous airport at Lukla, Nepal. Although not obvious in this photo, the runway is on a fairly steep incline, ending with a wall of rock just beyond the three white markings at the bottom of the photo.

A few images of the beautiful scenery we enjoyed while trekking through some of the lower elevation trails in Nepal.

On the second day of our trek up to Everest Base Camp, we stopped for a break while local porters passed by carrying supplies up the mountain. My friend Phil Sylvestro took this candid photo of one such porter, a young man likely still in his teens, carrying an unbelievably heavy and awkward load.

As impressive as human porters are in Nepal, yaks are on a completely different level. These respected, gentle giants are everywhere on the Himalayan trails, essential in moving goods up and down the mountain.

The village of Namche Bazaar in Nepal. We spent two days here acclimatizing to the altitude on our way up to Everest Base Camp. Namche is a stunningly beautiful and unique place, full of brilliantly coloured buildings and rooftops. This small village is nestled in a natural amphitheatre and is surrounded by the majestic Himalayan mountains on all sides. Namche may be the most meaningful and memorable place I have ever been.

This photo was taken during a training run on a steep slope above the village of Dingboche. We spent two acclimatization days in Dingboche before trekking further up the trail towards the villages of Lobuche and Gorak Shep. The mountain in the background is the beautifully impressive Ama Dablam.

The yak hut and rock enclosure pictured below, is near the Nha-La checkpoint, about forty kilometres into the race.

Trails and terrain in the region surrounding Nha-La, pictured above and below.

Mount Pumori, the highest peak in the above photo, as seen from the village of Gorak Shep. The two trails in the snow lead to the summit of Kala Patthar (seen in front of Mount Pumori), which provides an unobstructed view of Mount Everest. In the photo below, I am resting at the top of Kala Patthar with Mount Pumori in the background.

I love this photo of three of our mountain guides: Raj (left), Mindu (centre), and Eddie (right). I feel it perfectly captures the beauty and spirit of the mountains and the people of Nepal.

After meeting Chris (above) on my first day in Kathmandu, we embarked on separate trekking routes to Everest Base Camp before reconnecting ten days later.

Dole (above), and Machhermo (below), sites of some memorable training runs with Doug, Christine and Ruth.

The morning before race day at Everest Base Camp. It was a significant challenge to dig our tents out of three feet of snow and haul everything back down the trail to Gorak Shep.

A sudden snow storm at Everest Base Camp did not suppress the cheerful and positive attitudes of our guides and porters.

Ruth and I smile for the camera after a miserable night in our tent at Everest Base Camp.

My one and only photo of Ujesh. I was lucky to find it in a one second segment from my GoPro video.

It was on this trail that I encountered "yak sadness". Happiness returned about thirty minutes later however, as I met Ujesh.

Running in the brilliance of the morning sun brought on snow blindness that plagued me throughout the race.

The happiest point in my race probably occurred here, about one hour after my collapse at Thore.

These spectacular photos were taken by my Brazilian friend Robson Dantas as he stood part way up the slope of Kala Patthar on the morning of the race. The photo above is looking down at Gorak Shep, and the photo below is looking back towards Base Camp with the sun rising over Mount Everest.

These two photos were also taken by Robson, about thirteen hours apart. The top image of me is about five kilometres into the race, and below I am at the finish line, snow blind and sun burnt.

Back in Lukla two days after the race. One last photo with my new friends after spending three weeks together on the mountain.

(L-R) Raj, Mindu, Ruth, Christine, Eddie (kneeling), Douglas, North, Estelle (kneeling), Mark, and Murray

Sixteen

Yak Sadness

After the first uphill section near the start of the race, the trail levelled off for a few kilometres and within thirty minutes, I found myself separated from the faster runners ahead of me, and the slower runners behind me. I was completely alone and able to take in the beauty of the landscape surrounding me. The sun had now risen above the rugged horizon, the sky was a brilliant blue, and the mountains, which were completely snow-covered, reflected sunlight as if they were covered in diamonds.

This part of the course was one of the few relatively flat sections throughout the entire route, yet running along the narrow path of solid ice was extremely difficult. The trail that had been carved into the snow and ice was so slippery that my running pace was reduced to a cadence akin to that of an impaired driver walking heel-to-toe in a sobriety test.

The trail was also very narrow and the edges so hard and sharp that my ankles and shins would constantly scrape across the ice, causing me to wince in pain with every stride. And although the light on the snow had created one of the most majestic mountain views I may ever experience, the sun and its reflection was causing me to suffer from early stages of snow blindness. All of this with only five kilometres behind me and fifty-five still to go.

I ran for about an hour in these flat yet punishing conditions before arriving at the top of a long and steep descent that brings runners down to the small village of Dhukla. We had climbed up this section a few days earlier, and at the time, I was impressed with the magnitude of the rugged terrain ahead of us; the combination of car-sized boulders and steep incline was both imposing and daunting. I remembered Blair making specific reference to this part of the route when sharing stories of his Nepal adventure with me a few years earlier. The "Dhukla Defile" was the term he used to describe it, and he was incredulous upon hearing that I would be running down it.

Looking down from the top of this hill, the image I had in my mind from a few days prior was now something completely different. On that day the snow had yet to fall, and the surrounding mountains were partly obscured by cloud cover. Now the steep boulder field was covered in two feet of fresh powder and the mountains appeared to be rising right out of the trail. The sky was still cloudless and deep blue in colour, and the reflection of the sun off the 20,000-foot peaks displayed a level of clarity that accentuated every ridge and every contour; the beauty was breathtaking.

Standing in one spot and admiring the grandeur of the Himalayan Mountains is certainly a memorable "touristy" moment, but as a racer, movement is the only thing that matters, so down I went.

Descending the "defile" required me to literally bounce sideways from boulder to boulder in an awkward, exhilarating, and dangerous struggle to keep gravity from pulling me straight down the mountain. With every cautious step, I imagined myself slipping off a boulder and hurtling down the mountain in a human snowball, before crashing into the Dhukla teahouse at the bottom.

By the time I did safely reach the base of this hill, my legs were shredded, my eyes were burning, and my heart and lungs were screaming. I sat down to have a drink of water, and within a few minutes started to feel much better. The drop in altitude brought with it more oxygen, warm temperatures, and dry terrain—and most importantly, renewed energy and excitement.

***

THE NEXT TWENTY KILOMETRES of running were exhilarating: the trail remained dry, the ascents and descents were moderate, and the scenery was spectacular. For several hours, I ran alone and felt pretty good, this pain-free solitude allowing me the freedom to appreciate and enjoy mountain running at its most extreme. I was in a happy place.

Things started to change, however, as I approached a long and steep incline just a few kilometres before the place where I had stumbled into the "photo shoot" and where I had first met Ujesh. I hadn't been eating or drinking very much during the race, and along with my extended time at high altitude (now on my fifteenth day), fatigue from my struggles at Base Camp and Gorak Shep, and a mild headache brought on by the intense sun, I was starting to feel depleted.

Then an odd thing happened as I reached the top of this incline that added, in a strange way, to my mental fatigue. As I was walking up the hill and looking out beyond the summit, I noticed a large black prominence on the edge of the trail. All of the rocks throughout the area were various shades of grey, so something black appeared out of place. Once I reached the top of the hill, I saw that there were actually two large black objects and that they were definitely not rocks. It wasn't until I was standing directly beside the objects that I realized what I was looking at: two dead yaks!

There was something particularly disturbing about standing alone, in absolute silence, looking down at these lifeless majestic creatures. Perhaps more than anything else in the Himalayan Mountains, yaks are symbolic of the peaceful and magnificent world which I was in—and they are everywhere. Hearing the clang of their bells is almost meditative, and brushing past their slow, large, and imposing bodies on the narrow trails is awe-inspiring. After spending every day among these beautiful creatures, one can't help but think of them as large pets.

And just as with "real" pets, their death can affect people in significant ways, both mentally and physically. In my experience as an animal lover and pet owner, the hours and days after losing a pet can bring on feelings of complete weariness. Witnessing the death of a yak cannot equate to the death of my beloved dogs or cats, but something did happen to me at that moment that contributed to my growing state of exhaustion—exhaustion that would continue to get worse as I struggled for the next few hours, before collapsing at Thore.

***

FOLLOWING THE BOOST of energy from Sherpa Lady's tomato soup, Ujesh and I left Thore, and continued moving slowly until we arrived at our next stop, a small tent located at Nha-La. Nha-La was really nothing more than the name for a yak hut situated among a field of boulders along the banks of a river, but in this tent sat our doctor, who, although he'd been with our group for our entire time in the mountains, was simply known by all of us as just…Doctor!

By the time we reached Nha-La, I was feeling much better than I had at Thore, but my eyes were still burning and my vision was becoming worse. I had reached the tent within an hour of the cut-off time (after which, runners would be forced to spend the night, before finishing the race the following morning), so I was happy to know that I could continue on through the final twenty kilometres of the route and complete the race in one day.

The sun was now setting behind the mountains, and I was concerned about how my failing vision would impact my navigation and mobility on the trails. Doctor did a quick assessment of my eyes, administered a few eye drops (perhaps the same ones that I had given to Christine at Gorak Shep earlier that morning), and declared that I was fit to go. Ujesh and I crossed the river and headed back down the trail through the villages of Dole and Machhermo, on our way towards the finish in Namche.

Just as I had anticipated, darkness rendered me almost "blind," and I relied heavily on Ujesh for safety and guidance on the trail. As was the case earlier in the race, taps from Ujesh's umbrella continued to guide me away from the edge of the trail; running alone at this point would have been very hazardous.

I thought back to posters that we had seen regularly in teahouses throughout our trek about a hiker who had gone missing in this exact area. He, and others before him, simply disappeared and were never found—tragic, but not a surprise, for if one were to fall off the edge of the trail in this area, there would be no way they could ever be located in the valley below. These thoughts kept me very alert, if not a bit afraid.

In spite of my failing eyesight, I was actually feeling pretty good, and was able to run at a decent pace. It was uplifting knowing that the most difficult parts of the race were behind me, and that I was only about two hours away from Namche. Ujesh and I ran together silently as the sky grew darker and the air got colder. Eventually, the sound of the river became louder, and I knew that we would soon be approaching a hill that would lead us down to the lowest part of the course.

Once we had descended to the banks of the river, I looked up through the darkness towards a small light, then dropped my head in despair as I realized that we were now at the base of the very long and very steep Mong Hill. I had forgotten about this last obstacle on the course, and it was very demoralizing knowing that my triumphant run to the finish would now be delayed.

Ujesh and I began the slow climb up Mong Hill, while the exhilaration and renewed energy I had enjoyed during the previous two hours were once again gradually smothered by exhaustion and despair. As I placed one foot in front of the other, my only defense against a further slide back into a Thore-like depression was to think back to lighter and happier times when we had trekked through this same area earlier in the week.

Seventeen

Yak Happiness

While resting with Ujesh at the base of Mong Hill, I thought back to our trek, and the first night after departing Namche, where we had checked into a lodge in the Sherpa village of Khumjung. The lodge was beautiful, but the lady running the lodge was anything but! The Nepalese people we met on the mountain were almost without fail the most moral, happy, and loyal people I have ever met. This lady, however, was the lone exception.

Our "hostess" in Khumjung would take our money for various goods and services, but acted as if she didn't understand English; claiming to have no change, but promising that she would get it to us later—a "later" that never arrived. In particular, this was a significant annoyance for Doug and Christine.

They had paid for a shower earlier in the day, and the lady had said she'd give them their change later. That evening, Christine wanted to purchase some toilet paper, and asked that the payment be taken out of the change she was owed. The lady pleaded ignorance and wouldn't return the proper amount of money. After repeated attempts to reason with this woman, Doug and Christine finally let the issue pass.

This scenario repeated itself on one more occasion before it was my turn to deal with this manipulative lodge lady. I wanted to charge my phone and was prepared to pay her fee: 1100 rupees. I gave the lady 1500 rupees and asked for 400 in return. She took my money and then proceeded to play the confusion card as she tried to give me back only 200 rupees.

After witnessing the incidents earlier, I remained persistent in my demands for the proper change as my trekking mates looked on, laughing at her obvious attempt to defraud me. After this issue was resolved in my favour, I plugged in my phone and was able to connect with Sharon back home on FaceTime. As we were talking, the lodge lady interrupted me, saying I couldn't use the phone while it was charging. Then, of course, she asked for more money.

Despite her pleas and protestations, I managed to ignore the woman, and she finally retreated back into the kitchen, leaving me alone. This perfidious proprietor certainly created some frustrations, but also the silliness of her behaviour added some welcome comic relief for us all.

***

THE NEXT MORNING, we had departed Khumjung and begun the trek towards our next destination. As we were walking along one particular steep and winding section of trail, we came across a large yak that had slipped off the path and fallen a few metres down the slope, coming to rest with its hind legs tangled in a wire fence. It was struggling to get free and clearly in distress.

Without hesitation, Douglas, like some kind of Brazilian super-hero, scaled down the embankment, anchored his body against the yak's loins, and gently freed its entangled legs—all this while avoiding being impaled by the animal's immense sharp horns and flailing legs. It was an impressive feat indeed!

A few minutes later Douglas approached from behind, asking me in his broken English what would happen if he were to "sleep" on the trail? An odd question, I thought, but I gathered he was referring to "slipping" on the trail (just as the yak had) so I simply responded by telling him to be careful, and to try to lean towards the high side of the mountain.

Clearly, this was not the question he was asking as he continued, "No, Mark, I mean what about if I sleep earlier?" Another odd question, but being polite I asked him if he was OK, and replied with some encouragement for safe trekking on the trail ahead. With a bit of frustrated insistence he continued, "No, Mark, I mean how do you say when I sleep before now?" To my embarrassment, I finally realized he was simply asking me the correct way to say "slipped" (past tense) in English.

I loved this about Doug and Christine. They were always trying their best to speak English along the trek, even to the point of polishing their grammar. They had made a commitment to each other that, throughout the trip, they would always communicate with everyone and themselves in English, and never revert back to their native Portuguese. Such a charming couple!

FURTHER ALONG, we began the long descent down the notorious Mong Hill. Steep uphill sections are obviously difficult to climb, but this downhill section was shredding our legs like nothing we had encountered so far. With an incredibly long series of switchbacks, steep steps, jagged rocks, and dangerous drop-offs to the river valley below, descending Mong was punishing all of us.

We were all focused and very quiet at this point, with the only sounds being grunts emitted at regular intervals as each leg pounded down on the rocks below. It was not spoken, but I am sure all of my mates had the same ominous thoughts as I did about struggling UP this wretched hill eight days from now at the fifty-kilometre point of the actual race. Needing to release some tension, I asked out loud, "Is it any wonder why only SIX people in the entire world chose to run this fucking race?"

This brought some laughter from my friends as we continued the struggle down this seemingly endless wall of rock. Shortly after, some comic relief resurfaced again as I told Douglas and Christine that in Canada, we might call this "a real BITCH of a hill!"

"Mark, what do you mean by this word BEEETCH?" Douglas asked. Trying not to be too harsh, I replied that it was not pronounced "BEEETCH" but rather "BITCH," and that it was a bit of a derogatory term that is often used when cursing something or someone.

"But how is BIIITCH like the hill, Mark?"

"Well, Douglas," I replied, "it just refers to something really difficult or something you don't really like all that much."

"Oh," said Douglas, "so when I say I come from coastal Brazil and live in a BEACH city I should be careful not to say I come from a BIIITCH city."

Simple humour, yes, but at the time it was quite therapeutic. Finally, I told Douglas that the term actually describes a female dog, but is sometimes used when describing a woman with less than desirable qualities.

"Oh," Christine chimed in, "You mean the lady back at the lodge was a real BIIITCH."

I think they both finally got it.

AFTER A RELATIVELY SHORT TREK, we arrived at our next destination, the small village of Dole. Up to this point, I had been spending all of my time on the trail walking quite slowly. This highly restrained pace was necessary for proper acclimatization, but after a few days of trekking, I was anxious to do some actual running. I was thrilled when Doug and Christine asked me to join them for a short run after lunch.

The three of us slipped on our trail shoes, grabbed a water bottle, and headed up the slopes behind our teahouse. After about ten minutes of climbing, the trail came to an end, forcing us to either head back on the trail towards the site of the previously entangled yak, or continue forward and embark on some serious off-trail exploring. If I had been alone I probably would have turned back, but with three of us together, the physical and navigational challenges ahead seemed less daunting, so forward it was.

This was the first opportunity I had had to gauge what type of runners I would be competing against in the actual race. Up to this point I had assumed that, unlike me, anyone who decided to run a long-distance trail race at Mount Everest was likely to be a highly accomplished and competitive mountain runner.

Therefore—and with all due respect to my Brazilian friends—it was comforting to see that Doug and Christine were really…just like me: mediocre yet competent runners whose capability on technical mountain trails was just as much due to their adventurous spirit as it was to their experience and athleticism.

The three of us crested the first hill and began a gentle winding descent towards a river valley below. Once our view of Dole was behind us, the magnitude of the Himalayan range in front of us became increasingly more dramatic. With majestic 25,000-foot peaks towering above our heads and no trails below our feet, this running experience felt exotic. Prior to coming to Nepal, I had only participated in a couple of mountain races, with all of my mountain experiences occurring on well-marked trails. Now, running and scrambling through this remote Himalayan landscape with absolutely no guidance to indicate where I was going was exhilarating.

Before long, our trail-less travels had taken us far away from Dole, and none of us had any idea where we were, or how we would find our way back. Regardless, the sun was still high in the sky, the weather was perfect, and we all had water, so there was no real concern about being seriously lost. In fact, being a bit lost actually made me feel more intrepid and impetuous, so I picked up the pace, putting some distance between me and my friends.

As a physics teacher, I know that an increase in altitude corresponds to a decrease in gravity; objects actually weigh less as they go higher. Astronauts experiencing "weightlessness" in space is an obvious and extreme example of this phenomenon. Although I was running at an elevation that would have no perceivable effect on my weight, my euphoric state of body and mind allowed me to scramble across the rugged mountain terrain in a way that made me feel as light-footed as Neil Armstrong sprinting across the lunar surface!

My pace was now bordering on reckless, as I continued to bounce from rock to rock across a field of boulders that followed a gentle descent. Gentle soon gave way to steep, though, as I rounded a corner and found myself staring straight down a wall of loose rock; likely the result of a small avalanche. Danger and fear were distant emotions at this point, so I pushed forward with an even faster pace, intent on embracing every moment of this spectacular run.

The terrain was a mix of loose shale and large rocks, surrounding a gully that meandered to the valley floor below. For the next several minutes, my feet alternated from sliding down the loose shale to bouncing sideways off a fixed boulder to jumping sideways across the winding chasm. Near the bottom, the trail made a sharp turn, which I was able to navigate with the speed and agility of a quarter horse in a barrel race. This type of running was completely foreign to me and was pushing me to my limits—the experience was inspirational!

Eventually, the ground became flat, and I was able to stop and watch Doug and Christine continue their cautious scramble towards the bottom. Upon finishing their descent, Douglas' first remarks to me were "Wow, Mark, the Canadian Snake!"

I MUST ADMIT that on that day, I felt pretty damn good, and this rather odd compliment felt deserved and was appreciated. However, any vain thoughts I held of being some kind of accomplished mountain runner were short-lived, as the following day I joined Ruth for a run along the trails above the village of Machhermo.

Just as with Doug and Christine, this would be my first opportunity to see how my running ability would stack up against Ruth's. We started across the flat ground outside of our teahouse, then ran up a relatively gentle climb at a pace significantly faster than what I was comfortable with. I pushed a bit harder in an effort to keep up with Ruth, but I soon had to slow to a walk while gasping for air. Clearly, the pace I had maintained during my "glamour" run the day before was nothing like Ruth's. She continued to accelerate up the trail with remarkable ease, and within minutes was out of sight.

I kept running at my own moderate pace, and after about thirty minutes met Ruth on her way back from a turnaround a few kilometres ahead of me. Ruth's mastery of the high-altitude trails was impressive and inspiring. It served as both a reality check for me as to how "mediocre" I really was in this environment, as well as provided motivation to train smarter and harder. Ruth and I had now spent a week on the mountain together, quickly becoming good friends, and although I was feeling a bit deflated about my struggles, I was very impressed with Ruth and happy for her, as clearly she was destined to be among the leaders come race day.

As it turned out, Ruth did finish very strong in the race, and just two years after our time in Nepal, became a fixture on the highly competitive international trail running circuit. Her success quickly garnered sponsorship from industry icons like The North Face, Garmin, and Scott Running, and with their support she was able to leave her job as an English teacher in Taiwan to become a professional athlete.

Ultimately, Ruth's ability and work ethic propelled her to the top of the elite trail running world, where in 2018 she was crowned World Champion of the Golden Trail Series. I sometimes regret that I had not discovered trail running earlier in my life, and that perhaps I could have become more competitive and enjoyed some of this type of success. I realize, of course, that those days are gone, but to this day I often think of Ruth when training or racing, as I continue to push myself to become a better runner.

Eighteen

Back to Mong and Beyond

The happy memories from our pre-race trek eventually faded, and my attention once again turned to Mong Hill and the difficult climb that was still ahead of me. I tried desperately to find the strength to keep placing one foot in front of the other as Ujesh and I laboured up towards the tiny light of the Mong Tea House—1000 feet above us.

After recovering from my collapse at Thore and moving at a relatively rapid pace through the gentle slopes around Machhermo and Dole, I once again found myself in a state of physical and emotional exhaustion. Complete darkness had arrived and the fatigue, despair, and now a nocturnal version of blindness had returned. My Mong Hill struggle was turning out to be not only the most difficult part of the course, but without a doubt the most difficult experience of my life.

A few steps up the hill were followed by a few minutes of leaning on my poles while sucking in the thin air with heavy breaths. Ujesh's patience and quiet encouragement were the only respites from this predicament in which I found myself.

Partway up the hill I stopped once again, desperately trying to find the motivation to continue. It has always amazed me how, in every race, I constantly struggle with the desire to finish, while battling my mind's repeated efforts to rationalize quitting. At this point of the race, I wanted to finish more than I could possibly express, and I knew quitting was not an option: there was literally only one way out of this mess, and that was through. The finish line loomed over the back side of Mong Hill, but once again, just as in Thore a few hours earlier, I felt beaten by the mountain. Gravity seemed to be working overtime on me, and my legs and arms simply fell limp to the ground. Ujesh and I looked at each other, shut off our headlamps, and fell back against the mountain wall.

Night was upon us, the air was completely still, and the sound of my beating heart was loud enough to mute the cascading glacier river far below. I looked around through my bleary and burning eyes and could make out only three images: the distant light atop Mong Hill, the moon's reflection off the summit of the 25000-foot peak behind that Hill, and the faint glow from the eyes of Ujesh, once again regarding me with concern, as he had at every point since he'd taken on this journey with me.

I can't possibly explain it, but there was just something deeply mysterious and extraordinary about this humble and selfless human being that had a profound effect on me in that moment. Although our lamps were still shut off, I saw his silhouette approach and I heard those familiar words of his repeated: "Slowly, sir. This way, sir." The gentle confidence in his voice and the patience and care in his actions gave me the strength I needed to keep going. With that, our lamps were turned back on, silence returned, and Ujesh and I climbed steadily until the light of Mong Hill was at our backs, never to be seen again.

The rest of the way to the finish was not without its perils, as blindness made navigating the remaining few kilometres to the end almost impossible. My reliance on Ujesh and his umbrella was constant; taps to my elbow consistently kept me moving forward on the trail and safely away from the cliff's edge.

My head remained down for the rest of the race, following the blurred cadence of my feet below. And then, without notice, a building with a "Namche" sign appeared beside me, soon to be followed by the dark figures of locals cheering us on. Then a distant figure on the trail ahead waved a glow stick and blew a whistle, guiding me to the final turn to the finish line.

Ujesh and I made that final left turn down a set of steps toward the lights illuminating the finish line below, and twenty metres before the end I turned to my left to acknowledge and celebrate with the man who had run faithfully by my side for nine hours—only to discover that, just as mysteriously as he had appeared, he had now disappeared, leaving me to cross the finish alone.

The relief of those final few steps was beyond anything I had experienced in any other race, yet at the moment it somehow felt empty not having Ujesh by my side at the very end. Of course, his decision to fade away before the finish was totally consistent with his actions all along. It was my race, and his responsibility was to guide me safely to the finish; now, he had the sensitivity and the generosity to allow me to experience the culmination of this incredible journey by myself.

Hugs and congratulations from Ruth and our lead Sherpa, Raj, followed, as I stumbled to a chair to recover from my arduous journey. As I tipped my head back for a drink of water, there was Ujesh once again by my side, watching over me just as he had for the last nine hours. He said no words as I thanked him and gave him the few rupees I had remaining with me. And then, for the last time, he vanished, never to be seen again.

I will never see Ujesh or Sherpa Lady again, and they will never know anything more about me. However, if the human capacity for a sixth sense exists, I am hopeful that these two beautiful people will always sense how grateful I am to them and what they mean to me. I will NEVER forget either of them.

I chose to participate in this event to challenge myself—both physically and mentally. I feel that I met this challenge on both levels, and that my life will forever be better because of it. And although I went to Nepal on my own, the greatest part of this incredible experience was the opportunity to connect with people from around the globe who share my passion for this amazing part of the world, and my addiction to this crazy sport we call ultrarunning.

Everest will forever be etched into my memory, along with all the wonderful people I met: Douglas, Christine, Ruth, Murray, Estelle, Phil, Ujesh, Sherpa Lady, and all of our other Sherpas and porters. These people will be a part of me for the rest of my life. I am truly grateful to all of them for sharing their lives with me.

Nineteen

Why It All Matters

Without a doubt, my Everest adventure has assumed epic status in my life's story. However, throughout my years of running, I have come to realize that every event has been epic on some level.

Be it the danger and demands—both physical and mental—of Tromsø, the beauty and grandeur of Iceland, the pain and heartbreak of Leadville, or simply the daily escapes to my beloved Brandon Hills, running has blessed me with life-changing moments everywhere I have gone.

If asked to pick my favourite running experience, I would find it difficult to choose; everything I have done and everywhere I have gone in my running life has provided me with some form of unique and memorable moment. So when that question was posed to me recently by a fellow runner, I thought about everything running has done for me over the last ten years of my life, and concluded that Squamish and Montana were the two races that encompassed all that truly matters.

The Squamish 50 is a fifty-mile race on a highly technical course through the coastal mountains of western British Columbia. Squamish was one of the first "destination" races during my early days of trail running and in subsequent years I have been back for two more of these events.

The race director at Squamish is Gary Robbins, who is perhaps—excluding Kilian, of course—the most famous trail runner today. Although a world-class runner, Gary's fame stems less from his success on the trails than from his failures.

Over the last ten years, the Barkley Marathons (Laz's signature race) has become one of the most celebrated races in the world. Situated in the remote mountains of Tennessee, Barkley is a roughly one-hundred-mile race that is notoriously difficult, if not nearly impossible, to finish; the actual finishing rate over its entire history hovers at just over one percent!

Though Barkley accepts only a very limited field each year, Gary has managed to earn a spot at the starting line for three consecutive races. While he has failed to finish in every attempt, that in itself is not noteworthy, as in all of those three years combined there have only been two successful finishers. In a race that requires runners to complete five 20-ish-mile loops of the course, most don't even finish more than two.

In Gary's first attempt at a hundred-mile race with no course markings that runners must navigate on their own in under sixty hours, he made it to the final loop before his sleep deprivation produced disorientation that made him eventually get lost and unable to finish. This, again, is nothing special, as getting lost on a well-marked trail is common in ultra races (three times for me).

Really, the only thing that made Gary's DNF significant is that in recent years, despite its peculiar secrecy, Barkley has garnered a cult following and has been profiled on several popular documentaries. As the race's fame has grown, videographers and bloggers have become merciless in exposing Barkley failures every year.

So with one near-finish—and a very public failure—under his race belt, Gary was the one to watch when he returned to Barkley the following year, accompanied by his crew and a friend ready to document his attempt at redemption.

In this second attempt, just as in his previous race, Gary was one of only two runners to begin the final loop, which each runner must complete in opposite directions. After fifty-nine hours, and in pouring rain, the second runner arrived at the finish and tapped the famous yellow gate, becoming only the fifteenth person ever to finish Barkley.

As the clock moved closer to sixty hours, the large gathering of spectators and filmmakers were locked on the trail coming from the opposite direction, hoping to see Gary become the sixteenth finisher. At fifty-nine hours, fifty-nine minutes and thirty seconds, the crowd suddenly turned around...to see Gary approaching the finish line from the wrong direction.

With a final sprint over the last one hundred yards, Gary tapped the gate before falling to the ground at Laz's feet exhausted and in tears; the clock read sixty hours and six seconds! Just as in the previous year, Gary had once again become disoriented and lost on the final loop, resulting in perhaps the most legendary DNF of all time.

***

IN SPITE OF ALL HIS NOTORIETY, when Gary takes command of his race, he is no different from any other race co-ordinator and no different from any other trail runner; he just becomes a passionate, dedicated, enthusiastic fan of the sport. After the racers hit the trails, Gary makes his way to the finish line—where he remains for the entire day and night, giving big, sweaty, dirty hugs to every finisher.

Squamish has an electric and infectious spirit about it, and I love everything it has to offer. The field is always strong, the course is challenging and beautiful, and at fifty miles, it is the length of race that suits me best. Aside from most of the multiple long and steep climbs, much of the fifty miles is actually runnable, and over roughly half a day it provides me with the perfect combination of suffering and satisfaction.

One of the things I love best about mountain running is the way I approach steep downhill sections, which Squamish has in abundance. For some reason—and I can't fully explain this—I have always been able to let loose on downhills without trepidation or concerns about tripping and tumbling down the mountain. I have discovered, as was evident by my struggles with fear in Tromsø, that when fear is suppressed, mental and physical confidence takes over, and blasting down a rocky mountain trail can become a lot more fun and actually a lot more safe.

I recall in one of my races at Squamish, cresting the first steep climb of the day and stopping at the top to catch my breath and my wits before heading down the back side. This particular descent was very steep, very long, and full of rocks, roots, and fissures; just the way I like it. With a deep breath, a slap to the thighs, and a fist pump to the chest, I leaned into the abyss and let gravity do its thing.

My downhill style on challenging terrain like this is to employ a bit of an awkward- looking skip, hop and jump technique, whereby I actually gain a fair bit of air time between foot strikes. The sensation of free-falling down the hill and then sending rocks flying off the sides of my shoes is exhilarating. Just like when scaling up the Hamperokken summit, mind and body must be constantly focused on the task in order to avoid trouble or tragedy.

About halfway down this particular slope, I started to hear another runner behind me who was clearly employing the same "balls-to-the-walls" approach that I was. With the two of us blasting down the hill, rocks were flying everywhere while a chorus of grunts filled the air. It started to feel like this section of downhill constituted the entire race course, with the finish line at the bottom. The competitive nature in both of us seemed to rise as our paces became significantly faster, bordering on reckless. Finally, with one last leap, my feet struck flat ground, with my nameless friend right behind me. We both turned, looked up the mountain, and in perfect unison yelled, "that was freaking AWESOME!" These are the kinds of feelings that I can only get from trail running.

Later on in this same race, I found myself keeping pace with a runner from Greece who had recently arrived in Canada to take a job in Vancouver. Dimitrios and I would run together for a few kilometres and then part ways after each aid station before meeting up again several kilometres later. This pattern continued for most of the race, until we came down from the last mountain trail and started running together for the final few kilometres through the town of Squamish to the finish.

With about 500 metres remaining in the race, Dimitrios stopped and pulled out a large Greek flag from his Camelbak and draped it around his shoulders, in a clear display of national pride. As we approached the finish line, crowds of spectators began cheering for us and yelling, "Go Scotland! Woo-Hoo!" We looked at each other and laughed, Dimitrios shaking his head and murmuring, "Scotland? WTF? There's more than one country on this planet with a blue and white flag, ya know!" Dimitrios and I crossed the finish line together with fist pumps in the air, and then embraced as a race official announced over the loudspeaker, "Yeah, here's Mark and Dimitrios, making friends on the trail!"

It is just such an overwhelmingly satisfying and "cool" feeling to complete a race like this while sharing your joy with other runners.

Squamish was my first mountain ultra and after pushing through my first finish in about thirteen hours, I have been able to make significant improvements to my finishing time in each subsequent year, feeling stronger and happier each time. If the reason for competing in races is to be challenged, feel fit, and finish fast and happy, then Squamish has done that for me, and this is why I believe it represents mountain running in its purest form. Squamish makes me feel like a real mountain runner, and this is why I hope to keep going back until my body no longer can.

Beyond the significance of the race itself, one moment that will stay with me forever occurred shortly after my most recent race at Squamish. From the finish line, Sharon and I made our way across the street to a park where hundreds of people had gathered to watch and listen to a live feed of the iconic Canadian band The Tragically Hip's final concert.

"The Hip," as they are known to their adoring fans, were in their hometown of Kingston, Ontario to perform and celebrate the life of their founder and frontman, Gord Downie. Gord had recently been diagnosed with terminal brain cancer, but nonetheless had pushed through a gruelling cross-country tour battling pain, confusion, and exhaustion. Downie and his positive, gracious, and generous approach towards the end of his life had become a symbol of resilience and strength for Canadians across the country. Anticipation of the broadcast of his final concert had become as much of a unifying and patriotic event as anything in recent years. The Prime Minster was in attendance at the concert, and a massive Canadian flag made its way around the arena while teary-eyed fans joined together and screamed out the words to "O Canada."

Sharon and I joined the celebration on the edge of the park and stood silently, arm-in-arm, sipping on a beer. Onscreen, Downie belted out such visceral and appropriate tunes as "Courage" and "Tired as Fuck" while from the other side, cheers erupted as muddy, bloody, and exhausted runners continued to cross the finish line. The pride I felt in completing my most successful ultra race was now coupled with the pride I felt as a passionate Canadian. Few moments in my running life will ever be so poignant.

***

BIG SKY, MONTANA, a ski resort in southern Montana, is the site of my most recent mountain ultra, and is noteworthy for a few reasons. First, it is extremely challenging. At fifty kilometres, The Rut, as it is known, has exposed summits and ridges and has been part of the same Sky Running circuit as the Tromsø Sky Race; thus, it has always attracted the best runners from North America and beyond (Kilian raced here a few years ago…and won, of course).

Second, The Rut is really a mountain festival with races spread out over three days, and the event fills the streets with a combination of long hair, shaggy beards, puffy coats, and plaid.

One of the races during The Rut is the Lone Peak Vertical Kilometre (VK) which is run on the Friday of the Rut weekend. VK races are very popular in Europe, where they have their own competitive circuit, drawing a growing group of highly specialized athletes. Running a VK is like no other race, as the course must rise one vertical kilometre in elevation with no more than five kilometres in total distance; in simple terms this means that you are going up the entire way, with many sections requiring scrambling on all fours.

The Lone Peak VK starts at the base of the ski resort, and goes straight up to the 11,200-foot summit of Lone Peak. Lone Peak rises well above all other mountains in this part of the U.S. Rockies, and from a distance, has a look not unlike Mount Fuji in Japan.

In a relatively short running career, I have been able to pack in over 1000 kilometres of mountain races, but on race morning, this one kilometre looked more daunting than any other. Looking up from base camp, I could hardly believe that professionals were reaching the summit in only forty minutes. As the gun sounded and I started running, I had no sense of whether I could summit in even twice that time, or if it would take me much, much longer.

There have been a few of my races where the highest parts of the course are above the tree line, and the summit or pass that must be crested is visible for sometimes hours on end. It can be very discouraging to climb with the distant pass in sight, feeling like it will NEVER be reached; yet even though the annoying child-like chants in my mind of "Are we there yet?" never go away, the summit is somehow always conquered and painful memories soon fade.

Lone Peak was one of those races, as about halfway through, the summit seems to rise up a near-vertical wall of exposed, loose rocks, and never appears to get any closer. But before long, a small, weird community of volunteers and fans (including one guy who walked around the entire weekend wearing the same blond wig, tight gold shorts, and lime green "OREGON" sprinters singlet) start lining the course, yelling at runners, "Don't you dare stop, get to that (insert choice of profanity here) finish!" and within moments, as it always does, the climbing ends.

One hour and twenty minutes of running, climbing, scrambling and genuinely freaking out placed me in decent standing among the field, and as a runner, I have never been prouder.

Once they have finished the race, runners crowd into gondolas and chair lifts, which return them to base camp. During my return trip, I was nose-to-nose-to-nose with multiple finishers, including two extremely fit and muscle-bound shirtless young men from Alaska and Alabama.

"Alaska dude" was quite friendly and charming, whereas "Alabama Ahnold" was rather aloof and snobbish. Alaska remarked to Alabama that he was "right ripped" and commented that he must train hard to develop that magazine-cover body to help him grind up these punishing mountain races. As Alabama turned, with his granite-like deltoids brushing past my chin, his smug reply was, "Nah, I do it for the chicks."

Funny, yet a bit disheartening, that this "beefcake from the bayou" could display such an ego and such vanity, something I had never witnessed on the trails. In simple terms, he just seemed to be the complete antithesis of a genuine trail runner.

Trail runners wear mud and blood as badges of honour; shitting themselves during races and puking more frequently than eating serve as a clear indication that, on the trail, appearances are secondary. Alabama carried himself as I imagine someone would on the set of a shampoo commercial. All that seemed to matter to him was being noticed by others. He didn't even smell bad!

Upon our arrival at base camp, Alabama was quickly forgotten, while Alaska and I gave congratulatory slaps to each other's backs before he went his way and I made my way back to meet Sharon. The brief few moments I had shared with this kid, almost forty years my junior, was like a microcosm of so many things that I love about this sport: age, fitness, and finishing times really mean nothing on the mountain, as all that continuously shines on the trails is genuine respect and camaraderie among competitors. Of all the amazing memories I have taken from running events, it's these small bursts of bonding that remain with me more than all others.

LESS THAN FORTY-EIGHT HOURS LATER, I was back at the start line to compete in the fifty-kilometre race that would head back up to Lone Peak for one more punishing summit push. As is the case with almost every ultra race, we runners started very early in the morning, illuminating the trail with our headlamps.

To me, this has to be one of the coolest sights in all of sport: being halfway up a mountain trail, looking down and up and surrounded by hundreds of lights bouncing around in the darkness. On this race morning, and after about two hours in blackness on the trail, the headlamps faded as the sun began to rise, brilliantly illuminating Lone Peak as we ran below it. The beauty of the mountain was surpassed only by the pain in my stomach as I thought of grinding up that exposed ridge one more time about six hours later.

And what a grind it was. After about fifteen kilometres of some of my best trail running ever, I slipped on a rock and seriously twisted my ankle, reducing my "Kilian-esque" glide to a pathetic hobble. Things like this have happened before, where an injury strikes on the trail, bringing with it severe pain and restricted movement, but not bad enough to pull me off the course.

It is odd that, at times like this, I almost wish for the injury to be more serious, which would give me no choice but to disqualify myself. Such was not the case with my ankle on this day: it kept sending constant and almost unbearable streaks of pain from my foot up to my groin, but still allowed me enough freedom of articulation to delicately make my way through the rest of the course. The pain was bad—just not bad enough to quit!

In an odd way, making my second ascent of Lone Peak was actually somewhat therapeutic for my ankle, as the slow gait and axial stress on my legs from the solid rock and steep vertical minimized any real lateral strain.

Descending the mountain was a different experience altogether, though. The back side of Lone Peak transformed into a waterfall of loose shale, cascading all the way to the bottom and pushing every foot-strike sideways. This, combined with gravity doing its part to pull me straight down, made for an intensely painful and traumatic descent.

Finally, after a couple of hours in extreme terrain, the course gradually softened, allowing runners to glide downhill for five kilometres through gentle flowing single tracks, with a breathtaking mountain range in front of us the entire way to the finish.

Both the Lone Peak VK and the Rut 50 were incredible races, but not so incredible that I should have felt any more emotional in those races than I have anywhere else. I almost always have small, private, emotional moments at race finishes, but there was something about approaching this finish that brought on a tight stomach, a lump in my throat, and a flood of tears.

Perhaps it was the pride in conquering Lone Peak twice, or maybe it was the visceral relief of finally taking the weight off my throbbing ankle, or it could have been that I was successfully finishing a race that brought back such intense memories of Tromsø. But looking back, I believe it was the culmination of so many events like this: I have felt so fortunate at this point in my life to have been able to put my body and mind into a place that, just a few years previously, I would never have thought possible.

And now I was approaching the finish line, carrying all this physical pain and emotional intensity, with the greatest moment of all being the sight of my beautiful Sharon jumping and waving and screaming for me, as she does at every finish. On this day the sound of her voice and sight of her covered in sweat and dirt (from her own very demanding race in the mountains earlier in the day) brought out an emotional release that meant so much more to me than just finishing.

Embracing Sharon was symbolic of everything amazing that my running life has done for me. I had finally reached a level of greatness that mattered only to me, and the pride and conviction and camaraderie I had discovered on the trails had made their way into every part of my life. I had become a better person, and above all else, I knew at that moment I could have never reached this incredible place in my life without the love and support of the woman in my arms. I had finally come to see myself defined by ALL that I had embraced.

AFTER A FEW MOMENTS with my face on Sharon's shoulder, I felt a tap on my own. I pulled back from Sharon, only to turn around and see…none other than "beefcake" Alabama, his hand outstretched, handing me a beer. His eyes remained fixed on both me and Sharon as, without a word, his other hand gave me a gentle "well-done" pat on my back.

As we walked away from the finish, Sharon asked me who that guy was and if I knew him. When I explained the brief meeting we had had the previous day—and my less-than-positive first impression of him—she said, "I was wondering, because when he handed you that beer, I noticed he had a tear in his eye."

SO AS IT TURNED OUT, ole beefcake wasn't an asshole after all, and to others standing around the finish line, his act of kindness would have appeared rather ordinary. But at that moment, it was clear to me, that two ordinary trail runners had just shared something extraordinary.

A view of Lone Peak in Big Sky, Montana. The long ridge on the left leading up to the summit is the same ridge that is seen in the photo below.

Standing at the summit of Lone Peak and looking down the ridge towards the base of Big Sky Resort. I traversed this ridge and summited Lone Peak twice in the same weekend.

Sharon and I posing with celebratory antlers following our Rut Mountain Runs, and shortly after drinking my "beefcake" beer.

Waiting for the start of the Lone Peak Vertical Kilometer in Big Sky, Montana.

Congratulations from Gary Robbins at the finish line of the Squamish 50 race in Squamish, British Columbia, before heading across the street with Sharon to join in the celebration of the Tragically Hip's final concert.

Twenty

Ultra Distancing

Since my last race some six months ago and the writing of the words on this page, much has conspired to shape my running future.

A brisk fall run through the forest with my squirrel-obsessed dog tied to my waist ended abruptly, as an unfortunate combination of slick mud and a lunge towards a rambling rodent dropped me awkwardly to my knees, covering me in a lot of mud, a little blood, and leaving me with a torn meniscus.

A few months later, along the same trail in the early winter, a leisurely early-season ski was also painfully interrupted when a small hill and a tight turn forced my legs to spread apart on an uncontrollable and painful trajectory, impaling me on a wire fence and leaving me with a second torn meniscus.

Around the same time, I was also diagnosed with a painful lower back condition that restricted movement, as well as a myriad of arthritic and nerve afflictions. Two orthopedic surgeons advised me that although my knee and back injuries were not serious enough for surgery, they would likely NEVER heal, and their advice was to simply continue with athletic therapy and discontinue ultra running!

Ultra running distances are not clearly defined, like the standard 26.2-mile marathon is, so I decided to "sort of" follow the advice of the medics and restrict my race pursuits to fifty miles or less, while increasing my time at the gym in an effort to stabilize my ailing limbs and torso.

With the arrival of spring, a rigorous gym routine, and an ambitious running training plan, my anticipation for late spring and early summer races was building. Then an insidious bug from a bat abruptly shut down the planet, taking with it every gym and every race scheduled for the next four months (or…much longer).

Without a gym to train in or a race to train for, my commitment to running fell victim as well. Thankfully, as one race after another was cancelled, online running platforms became flooded with motivational strategies to encourage everyone to stay interested, stay focused, and stay committed to alternative running and wellness pursuits in order to fill the void in every runner's race calendar. One day, a notice appeared on the Facebook page of Personal Peak, a company in Alberta that provides coaching services to runners, about plans for an actual race that could be run in one's own backyard: The Quarantine Backyard Ultra!

THE QUARANTINE BACKYARD ULTRA, the brainchild of Dave Proctor (the director of my previous Backyard race in Alberta), would follow the same format and rules as other Backyard events, with the lone exception being that the race would not be run in one location, but rather at each racer's actual home. Home, by this definition, could be any 6.71-kilometre route that would begin and end at one's actual house.

Runners were given the option to complete the distance outdoors, around a 6.71-kilometre loop (or a series of shorter loops), or indoors on a treadmill (or some other creative way of covering the distance inside a house). As in all Backyard races, this distance had to be completed every hour, with the next "lap" beginning at the top of each subsequent hour.

All runners would set up a camera at their start area, which would then be connected to a live video stream on Zoom. Warning whistles and start bells would signal to runners around the world to begin their laps at exactly the same time, and when they finished their lap, runners would display their GPS device to the camera to verify the completion of the required distance, and then upload their data to Strava.

When I first read about this event, my interest was mild at best, but as race day approached (only about two weeks after the initial announcement), my excitement and anticipation began to build. By race morning, my stomach was turning as much as it would have been if I were toeing the start line at Leadville or Boston. Running alone, basically around the block on icy sidewalks for hours on end, would hardly make it onto my "Greatest Hits" list but, as the hours passed, what began simply as a fabricated reason to go for a competitive run soon evolved into something much bigger.

My day, as it turned out, amounted to nothing extraordinary. After an early spring thaw and mild temperatures two days earlier, a major storm arrived, bringing mid-winter temperatures along with snow and ice to my race route. Running in these conditions was far from pleasant, with the only remotely interesting part of the race being the return to my house every hour, where Sharon diligently fed me everything that a runner could possibly put on his "most-wanted" list.

My cache consisted of perogies, sausages, cheeseburgers, ham sandwiches, Kraft Dinner, Zoodles, chocolate bars, chocolate cake, orange pop, potato chips, and cookies. And although the desire was strong to keep running so I could continue to eat all the garbage that I normally don't, after thirteen hours my battered knees finally brought my race to an end—but, ironically, that's where my real interest in it began.

WHEN THE QUARANTINE BACKYARD ULTRA was first announced I, and I assume many other runners, perceived it as a bit of a gimmick, with no legitimate attraction for the running community at large. However, once Dave and the race organizers started putting the word out to well-established, seriously competitive runners, global interest spread like a virus in Hokas.

Before long, over 2400 runners from over fifty countries had signed up for the race, and the elite field of participants read like a list from the future running Hall of Fame. At least twenty world-class runners had made a commitment to the race, including champions from some of the world's most challenging and famous races.

All of these running celebrities would be on the live Zoom feed for their entire race, giving the viewing public an opportunity to have a peek at their real lives and to appreciate their real personalities. In the vacuum of live sporting events, some serious media outlets like Sports Illustrated and The New York Times even jumped on board to cover the event.

When the event began, there was Courtney, ranked among the top ten ultra runners of the last decade; after running each loop, she recited jokes from her book, 500 Hilarious Jokes for Kids, to the adoring Zoom audience. Given her prodigious abilities, we knew that if she were to read just a few jokes each lap, it was not inconceivable that she would need to find another book to read before her race was done.

She had, after all, finished as runner-up at Big's Backyard Ultra two years earlier, running for sixty-seven hours and almost 450 kilometres! However, after twenty-four hours and 100 miles, Courtney, along with her jokes, signed off from the Zoom feed with the send-off, "Yeah, a hundred miles is enough for today!"

Well past thirty hours, another runner, Sarah, took the stage from Courtney, continuing with her own brand of lame jokes:

"What do you call a runner with no shins?"

"Tony!" Or:

"How did the mathematician deal with his constipation?"

"He worked it out with a pencil!"

Even Laz, who, along with his wife Sandra, was part of the live stream for most of the race, chimed in with some of his own hillbilly humour:

"How do you know the toothbrush was invented in Alabama?"

"Because if it was invented anywhere else, it would be called a teethbrush!"

Jamil, or Jam-Jam as he is known to his popular YouTube audience, sat in front of his camera and answered questions from Zoom viewers after each lap. About halfway through his day, Jamil moved from running loops outside his home to completing each hour on his treadmill...set at an incline of 40 degrees! Jam-Jam pulled out of the race before completing twenty laps, but he could be forgiven for not going farther, as a few days earlier he had completed a marathon by running circles around a helicopter pad on top of his office building.

A fan favourite before and during the race was Anna, yet another world-class athlete, who ran her race on a frozen lake in the Swedish Arctic. At the end of each lap, she warmed up in what looked like a crudely constructed Sami hut from Lapland. After over forty hours, Anna disappeared from the live stream, leaving her online followers worried for her safety. Shortly after, however, reassuring messages appeared on Facebook indicating that Anna had had to pull out of the race due to an approaching blizzard and a shortage of fuel for her cabin generator.

Along with Dave, who alternated between running laps on a treadmill inside and a route outside, another accomplished Canadian runner, Matt (the last runner standing in the Outrun Rare Backyard), was still in the race after thirty hours. When Dave was forced out with a back injury, Matt found himself among the final six runners, and (for good reason) had become the focus of online followers. Partway through the race, Matt was forced to abandon the route outside his Alberta home due to dangerously cold conditions. His crew immediately improvised and established a new route inside a local coffee shop, where Matt continued to run in sock feet around a pile of stacked-up tables and chairs, before dropping out of the race after forty hours.

Earlier in the race, interest in Matt had been largely overshadowed by a then-unknown man from Dubai who ran for over twenty hours around his living room couch! The "Living Room Guy," as he became known, evolved into somewhat of a celebrity after quickly garnering a very large YouTube audience—as a result of an online crusade mounted by fans that prompted the organizers to include his Zoom feed among those of the elite field.

There were many stories from the day that captivated the live stream followers. First there was Greg, one of a handful of runners still going strong after forty hours, who earlier in the day had had to step away from his treadmill twice: once to help euthanize a goat (yes, he does live on a farm) and a second time to remove a snake from his house.

Then there was Ben, a thirteen-year-old boy, who ran the race with his father. Ben's Dad decided to quit after six hours, but Ben himself chose to keep going, and continued running alone for another eighteen hours, finishing the day accumulating over one hundred miles!

There was Harvey, another superstar ultra runner, whose Zoom feed was pointed outside his kitchen window in the direction he would be running, with a live stream of pretty much nothing until he came into view at the end of each lap. Harvey did suddenly capture the audience's attention, however, when after leaving the house on one of his laps, his dog jumped out through the open window to join him in running around the neighbourhood.

And then there was Olivier, a U.S. National 24 Hour Run team member who, between laps, sat down to a live feed of himself dining on a plate of seared foie gras accompanied by a glass of Bordeaux Grand Cru!

ULTIMATELY, THOUGH, the story that really mattered to the growing audience was the one played out by the final two runners: Mike, an American record-holder in multiple long-distance events, running loops around his neighbourhood; and Radek, an equally impressive yet relatively unknown athlete, running on his treadmill in Prague.

After Anna from Sweden dropped out of the race as the third-place DNFer, Mike and Radek continued in tandem for the next sixteen hours. During this time, and accompanying the live feeds of both runners, race organizer Travis (who may have gone without sleep through the entire event), and the combo of Laz and Sandra provided both intentional and unintentional commentary.

One moment, Radek would be talking to Travis about the brand of tea he was drinking or mentioning that he had bought his treadmill only one week prior to the race; the next moment, audio would switch to Laz and Sandra as they rambled on, apparently unaware they were live, about baking cookies and preparing their income taxes.

During the race's fiftieth hour, however, the live YouTube stream was suddenly shut down because music playing in the background of someone's Zoom feed had violated a copyright agreement. Travis and his team managed to quickly migrate the Zoom feed to their Facebook page, where the focus on the final runners, along with commentary from Laz and Sandra, began to generate a massive following of viewers and their comments—some serious, some silly.

For many hours viewers, whether because of their own sleep deprivation and/or consumption of Bordeaux, became obsessed with a set of orange traffic cones set up in front of Mike's start corral. At one point one of the cones got knocked over, which sent the online viewership into a frenzy (although the following quotes are not necessarily verbatim):

"Someone PLEASE rescue that cone; it is so disrespectful to leave it floundering like that!"

"Holy crap, did you see that truck drive by? It almost flattened that poor cone!"

"Someone out there, please ask Mike to pay that cone some respect and run a lap with it!"

"Hey, does anyone know what model of Hokas Mike is running in?" "Yeah," replied another online viewer, "Hoka Cone Cones!" (for those who don't know, this was wordplay on the name of the actual shoe model, Hoka One Ones)

At one point a group of kids actually ran their bikes over the cone, crumpling it even further, prompting outrage from the Cone Fan Club:

"WTF, who do those little buggers think they are, crushing that cone?"

Disdain for children was thankfully short-lived, though, as moments later a charming infant entered the field of view, and began dancing around the cones in a truly poignant moment:

"Oh, that sweet child is performing a dance to the cone gods, bringing strength and good fortune to Mike during these challenging times!"

VERY SILLY STUFF for sure, but I—and many others—couldn't stop following this extremely "boring" yet remarkably captivating story. As the race approached its sixtieth hour, the tone of the online viewership became markedly more serious. The flood of Facebook comments were now focusing on the race itself and the competitive battle that was being played out in front of them. Pro-Mike and pro-Radek camps were becoming evident and supporters began questioning rules and records.

Some questioned whether Radek's now well-used treadmill could possibly be recording accurate data after sixty hours of continuous use, while others raised the concern that the ever-increasing number of people wandering along or through Mike's route violated the genuine Backyard restriction of no support for runners once they were on the course.

After the start bell for several of the laps, fans noticed that even though Radek was standing on his treadmill, several seconds would pass before he started moving—a clear rule infraction. Even Laz was overheard commenting to Sandra that Radek was not following the rules. In spite of all of this analysis, viewers were united in urging both runners to continue for several more hours, as they were approaching the Backyard record of sixty-eight hours.

By this time in the race, my last lap had ended almost fifty hours earlier, but I too was now caught up in the hype and couldn't stop watching. It was fascinating to witness how something that started as simply a challenge to a bunch of house-bound runners to go out and jog a few laps around their neighbourhood was now becoming a global phenomenon. I was captivated!

AFTER STEPPING AWAY for a few moments, I returned to the live feed a few minutes into lap sixty-three, with Mike already out on the course and Radek ambulating on his treadmill, as he had done for the previous sixty-two laps. However, during my absence, I learned that Radek had apparently started moving on his treadmill more than a full minute after the start bell.

I caught a quick glimpse of Laz leaving our field of view followed by a clearly audible pronouncement:

"He didn't start on time, the race is over!"

Moments later, the race clock switched to a view of Travis, completely quiet and looking straight down and away from the camera. He lifted his head and then began crying while he explained (and apologized) that he was disqualifying Radek for the late start to his lap. Travis was clearly distraught over this situation and was emotionally torn by making the decision to end a race that had captured the world's attention, and one that everyone wanted to see continue.

Comments from Facebook followers now shifted from the runners to Travis, with reactions ranging from agreement and support for the disqualification to anger and disgust with Travis and his organization for showing such blatant disregard for both runners.

As disturbing as it was to view these latter comments, it was not unexpected. After investing the time I had in running and watching the race, I felt no small measure of empathy for those who commented. What was obvious to me, and likely everyone else who had found the live feed absorbing, was that this experience had become deeply personal to so many people affected by the Covid crisis.

The Quarantine Backyard Ultra had become an escape, an indulgence, and a moment of joy. Those of us around the world who had spent the better part of three full days following it quite simply did not want the experience to end. The end of the race meant a return to the monotony, isolation, and loneliness of life that had been smothering many of us for the last few months.

Yet as time went on and the harsh comments began to be retracted, the running community began to realize that, regardless of personal opinions on the disqualification, a race born out of isolation and separation had provided all of us with an experience that became more social and more exciting than anything most of us had enjoyed in a long time. What started as a rather ordinary event had evolved into an extraordinary experience, one where sadness and happiness had merged into a very powerful and visceral emotional moment, and I will forever be thankful to have been part of it.

Afterword

I don't consider myself to be a serious globetrotter, but I do feel fortunate, if not privileged, that trail running has taken me to many amazing places throughout North America and beyond. I have always been drawn to mountains, but until running entered my life, opportunities to explore high altitude trails would have been rare.

Travelling across the globe, to enjoy and endure some of the world's most challenging and spectacular mountain terrain, became my inspiration for writing this book. Through my eyes, these adventures have been exotic and epic, and hopefully, sharing them with you, the reader, has been a worthwhile undertaking.

Everywhere I have travelled and raced has blessed me with a lifetime of memories, and I am hopeful that in a post-Covid world, I will be able to continue exploring the planet and seeking out more mountain challenges. Yet, if I were to choose one place in the world that offers me the most complete and most fulfilling trail running experience, it might be right here in Manitoba. This is not a statement that is clouded by "hometown pride"; it is an honest assessment of the challenging, beautiful, and varied terrain that this province has to offer.

A view of the Souris River valley, while running along the equestrian trails in the Souris River Bend Wildlife Management Area.

Stopping for a break at Bald Hill with my dog Stella, while running through the East Escarpment trail network in Riding Mountain National Park.

There are many beautiful scenes throughout the Canadian prairies, but few can match a winter sunset over a frozen lake, seen here along the North Shore trail in Riding Mountain National Park.

One of my favourite places to run, anywhere: the "blue car" trail in the Brandon Hills.

An early spring thaw along the Epinette Creek trail in Spruce Woods Provincial Park.

Ask any trail runner, be it a local slogger or an international sensation, what they seek out in a trail running adventure, and their reply would likely include: winding single-track trails that demand technical control, lots of elevation gain with leg-shredding hills, canopies of trees that provide protection from sun and wind, opportunities to encounter local wildlife, moments of beauty that stop runners in their tracks, and virtual isolation from any other human being. Manitoba offers the trail runner all of these experiences.

THE BRANDON HILLS, a Wildlife Management Area only a few minutes from the city of Brandon, is home to the trails that I frequent the most. It is a vast, forested network of trails that is a year-round playground for the casual hiker or the hard-core adventurer seeker. Narrow, gnarly, and undulating single-track trails seem to go on forever —it is a true hidden gem.

Just a short drive beyond the Brandon Hills is a forested river valley known as the Souris Bend. This stunningly beautiful region, which is managed and maintained by a local equestrian association, encompasses a series of trails that present runners with multiple river crossings and climbs that are steep enough to reduce the most skilled mountain runner to a turtle-paced grind.

Drive forty minutes from Brandon and the trail runner will find themselves in Spruce Woods Provincial Park, an area so unique that a similar region may not exist anywhere else in North America, if not the world. Glacial melting has deposited vast quantities of sand over this relatively small area and could make one think they had been transported to an Egyptian desert. Among the expansive sand dunes lay multiple stands of aspen and spruce forests that challenge the trail runner with enough cumulative elevation change to make one's legs feel like they are power hiking in the Himalayas.

Throw a hot cup of coffee in the car and head north out of Brandon; by the time you reach the vast boreal forests of Riding Mountain National Park, you'll still be enjoying a warm brew. Riding Mountain offers up the most expansive and varied trail running opportunities in the province, and in fact Tourism Manitoba should strap a GoPro onto a staffer's chest and send him out on a twenty-kilometre run through the extreme terrain of the East Escarpment. Circulating that video out on the Web would draw adventure seekers from across North America—it is that good!

And these areas are by no means the end of the line for trail runners in Manitoba. The recently constructed Northgate trail system completes a string of at least ten different forested trails that branch off of the fifty-kilometre highway connecting the southern and northern boundaries of Riding Mountain Park. Drive an hour beyond Northgate, and you will be immersed in the remote beauty of Duck Mountain Provincial Park and, just a bit farther, the Porcupine Hills Provincial Forest. Heading south towards the American border will bring runners to yet another entry into Manitoba's web of natural attractions, the rolling hills and trails of Turtle Mountain Provincial Park.

What is remarkable is that all of the world-class trails that I have just described are packed into my small corner of southwestern Manitoba. If one has the time to embark on a slightly longer journey, just ninety minutes east of Winnipeg, and still only a few hours from Brandon, they will be rewarded with perhaps the most rugged and challenging terrain in all of Manitoba—the remote and rocky trails on the edge of the Canadian Shield.

If you were to talk with any trail runner anywhere in the province, they would surely add to the list of exceptional running trails that may be found in their own backyard; there's no doubt that Manitoba is an absolute runner's paradise.

The "grass is always greener" credo can relate to many things. Exotic and adventurous destinations are captivating to all of us, but once they are experienced, our appreciation for what we have at home becomes even more captivating. Sipping from a glass of France's finest Pinot Noir along the vineyards of Burgundy is an exotic indulgence by any measure, but nothing really beats a cold beer on a hot summer day in my own backyard. Similarly, offer me the opportunity to jet off for a running vacation through the mountain trails of Patagonia and my Salomons and I would be there in a heartbeat, but if I were told that the rest of my running days would be confined to the trails within a three-hour drive from my home—well, I would still consider myself to be as fortunate as any runner across the globe.